POST CARD HAWAI

Hi
Greeting from Waikiki,
hope you're doing well. We
are enjoying our stay here.
Wish you were here.
Look forward seeing
you soon!

Ho
6   Transylvania Lane

Umbre, Romania

C000228262

Aloha
FROM
HAWAII

Wish You
Were Here

Sony Pictures Animation

Presents

THE ART OF
HOTEL TRANSYLVANIA 2

FOREWORD BY
GENNDY TARTAKOVSKY

—

WRITTEN BY
BRETT RECTOR

—

DESIGNED BY
IAIN R. MORRIS

TITAN BOOKS
London

PAGE 1: *Monster Ball soup* • Chin Ko
PAGES 2-3: *Camp Winniepacaca* • Miguel Gil
PAGES 4-5: *Vlads' castle* • Joey Chou
BELOW: *Hotel lobby screens* • Joey Chou
BOTTOM RIGHT: *Bigfoot CD* • Joey Chou
RIGHT: *Cubist painting* • Todd Gibbs

Be Sure To Play Our Thrillin[g]

GOLF COURS[E]

" The Greatest Water Haza[rd]
This Side Of The
Bermuda Trian[gle]

While in
Transylvania,
Be sure to visit historic

Downtown Pytovka

For Great
Shopping,
Fine **Dining**
and
Certain Death.

see concierge for more information

PYTOVK[A]

On Sale
in the Hotel Gift shop

[O]LD WORLD DIRT

Give That Coffin Back Home The
"Transylvania Touch"

GIFT CERTIFICATES | NOW AVAILABLE

BIG FOOT
A Walk
In my shoes

an
Autobiography

CONTENTS

FOREWORD BY GENNDY TARTAKOVSKY

Mel Brooks walked into the recording studio and I instantly got the flop sweats! When I immigrated to America from Russia I was seven, and TV in Russia had very minimal programming. Upon our arrival my father bought a little TV and I discovered the plethora of TV shows, cartoons, and movies that would shape my sensibilities into what they are today. *Young Frankenstein*, *Blazing Saddles*, *High Anxiety*, *History of the World Part 1*, and *The Producers* were my comedic pillars growing up.

Mel is almost 90 years old, and I wasn't sure what to expect. Would he still be the vibrant, witty comedian, or someone whose age had caught up to him? Well, he came in and was in fact everything that I thought he would be: funny, jovial, sarcastic, and larger than life. Directing someone of his talent and experience is probably the easiest or hardest thing I've ever done. On one hand, he needs no directing, he understands the intent and the joke and delivers it effortlessly, but there are some cases when it needed to be different than what he was doing. I gently asked him to do another take. He stared back at me with an uncomfortable silence.

"How would you say it?" he asked me. As if I wasn't sweating enough already! I felt the little beads form on my forehead. How am I ever going to do a line reading for MEL BROOKS?! I reached deep into my mind and turned off all my fear and insecurities and just casually acted out the line the way I heard it. Mel stared at me again with that awkward silence and said...

"Okay I'll do it your way, ONCE." He was sarcastic of course and I laughed uncomfortably, wiping the sweat from my brow.

Recording with Mel Brooks was one of my highlights in making *Hotel Transylvania 2*. Crafting an animated movie is a physical and mental challenge and it's the people that you surround yourself with that keep you going through the good days and dark days. And sometimes it's the opportunities like working with a legend like Mel Brooks that really keep your enthusiasm up.

In the 20-plus years that I have been working I have formed many long lasting relationships, and the ones that have blossomed at Sony Pictures Animation I'm sure will be with me through the rest of my career. This book has a lot of great art and I hope you enjoy looking at it as much as I did when I saw it for the first time.

INTRODUCTION

"Part of what makes the Hotel Transylvania movies so fun is we have the option to go for a bigger range with our characters. Even though it's really pushed sometimes, and there's lots of variety, it all stays in the same realm. Because everything comes from the director, there's a consistency to the style that's maintained throughout."
— ALAN HAWKINS · ANIMATION SUPERVISOR

IN *HOTEL TRANSYLVANIA 2*, audiences are once again invited to walk through the doors of the world's premiere five-steak resort for monstrous fun and whimsical mayhem. As the coffin lid opens on the latest vacation, director Genndy Tartakovsky and his talented production team invite audiences to celebrate the wedding of Dracula's daughter, Mavis, to the wonderfully sweet human Johnny, and, subsequently, the arrival of their son, Dennis.

In honor of these momentous occasions, the entire gang once again comes to visit—Frank, Eunice, Wayne, Wanda, Murray, Griffin, and even the Blob (affectionately known as Blobby) are all accounted for. And since the hotel now caters to human guests as well, Johnny's family also makes the trek to Transylvania to witness events no one thought possible!

In *Hotel Transylvania*, Dracula struggled to overcome his prejudice toward humans and allow his daughter Mavis to explore a world he had perceived as uninviting and dangerous to monster-kind. He learned that humans actually love monsters and relish in celebrating them, prompting him to have a change of heart and finally let humans into his life.

Hotel Transylvania 2 builds upon this change by highlighting the contrast that exists between the monster and the human worlds.

It's less about a fear of one another and more about defining what should be considered "normal." When it appears that Dracula's grandson, Dennis, is going to be a human instead of a monster, the question arises as to whether he should be around people who are more like him. Johnny and Mavis plan a trip to Santa Cruz, Johnny's hometown, giving audiences their first view of life outside Transylvania.

To dramatize the contrast between the monster and human worlds, production designer Michael Kurinsky and his team of artists used color and lighting to illustrate the differences. Whereas the monster world features structures built using a tall, monolithic shape language and a bright, saturated color palette, the human world contains structures made using a horizontal, flat shape language and a bland, de-saturated color palette. Furthermore, color and lighting play a critical role in establishing the aesthetic or mood of a particular scene throughout the production.

Another important area of artistic emphasis was character animation. Audiences will be delighted to see that Tartakovsky once again inspired his crew to achieve the signature "pushed" animation style that was perfected in the first movie. Everything in the world of *Hotel Transylvania 2* is just as much, if not more, cartoony and caricatured. But this pushed animation style is more than just a crowd pleaser. Tartakovsky's approach to the style challenged his animators to take onscreen actions in bold directions so that everything moves or behaves in unique, specific ways, rather than defaulting to the tired tropes of realism.

The only time there is a hint of realism is when Dracula makes the trek to his dad Vlad's underground lair, where Bela, Vlad's number two, and his other cronies make their appearance. The team employed a new technique to build an actual muscle system underneath the skin of these characters, adding just a touch more menace to the fiendish newcomers. While this was a first for the franchise, and something Tartakovsky tends to shy away from, the results add another spectacular visual dimension to an already richly stylized movie.

To guide us through this journey, the creative masterminds at Sony Pictures Animation have once again assembled a comprehensive tome displaying the vibrant world they created. So now, weary traveler, it is time to call for room service, place the Do Not Disturb shrunken head on the door, and relax as you begin your imagination vacation in the world of *Hotel Transylvania 2*.

ABOVE & OPPOSITE: *Final frames*
OPPOSITE TOP: *Dracula and Mavis painting* • Seonna Hong

DRAC'S PACK IS BACK!

WITH MAVIS AND JOHNNY'S NUPTIALS on the horizon, some familiar faces from the first movie are poised to make their return to Dracula's popular ghoulish getaway. Frank, Eunice, Wayne, Wanda, Murray, Griffin, and even Big Foot and the Blob— or Blobby, as he is affectionately referred to—have all booked rooms at Hotel Transylvania.

While they've been away from the hotel, a few monsters have made names for themselves outside the creepy confines of the monster world, now that humans universally accept monsters and vice versa. Even though there isn't a "montage of what all of Dracula's friends are up to now," says producer Michelle Murdocca, "we know that Frank has penned an autobiography; Murray has turned into a fashion designer, and actually served as a judge on a *Project Runway*-like show; Griffin has starred in a series of workout videos; and Big Foot has become a

sensation in the elite German soccer league. As for Wayne, he's become a tennis instructor of sorts at the hotel . . . that is, when he and Wanda aren't busy taking care of their litter, which has increased twofold."

"As far as the overall look of the characters is concerned, they're already iconic. People are familiar with Johnny, Mavis, and Dracula."
— MICHAEL KURINSKY · PRODUCTION DESIGNER

HEEEERRREE'S JOHNNY! AND THE FAMILY, TOO!

D ISCUSSIONS ABOUT DESIGNING Johnny's family started with his parents, Mike and Linda. However, before the production team could really begin to create their look, they had to nail down who they were.

Initially, there was a lot of talk about each family member's personality. Are they all like Johnny—slightly offbeat and living on the edge—or something altogether different? "When we were first designing the mother, Linda, we thought she might be a little more like Johnny, which is to say a little more kooky—someone who wore a lot of big bracelets and bright clothes," explains production designer Michael Kurinsky.

After much consideration, the team abandoned the idea of making the parents like Johnny and went in another direction, opting to play the parents as a straight-laced, typical suburban couple. "Knowing that Nick Offerman and Megan Mullally were going to provide the voices took everything to another level. Their comedic talents really helped mold their characters," says director Genndy Tartakovsky.

Linda is described as "very dry, sarcastic, and condescending. She will always politely call people out on what she perceives as a shortcoming, in a sweet-as-pie voice, of course, " says producer Michelle Murdocca.

"She's a little like Eunice, but she's not as brash," adds Tartakovsky. "Everything she says carries an implied insult, despite the fact it comes out super nice."

ABOVE: *Halloween portrait* • *Michael Kurinsky*
ABOVE RIGHT: *Graduation portrait* • *Seonna Hong*
BELOW (LEFT TO RIGHT): *Johnny's Dad* • *Craig Kellman, Stephen DeStefano, Andre Medina*

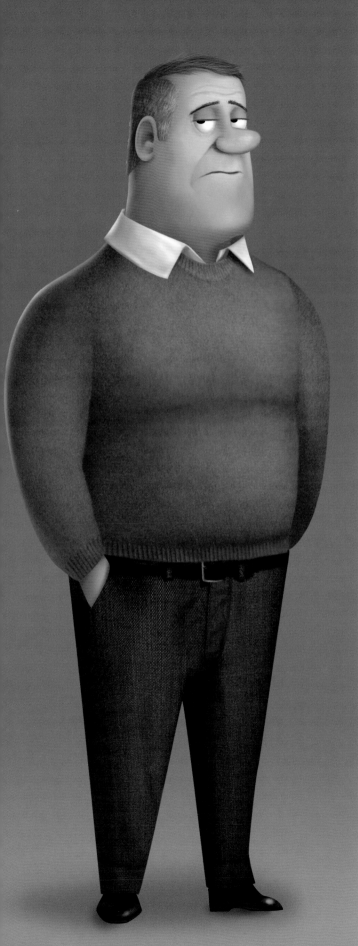

Johnny's Mom

Far Left: *Johnny's dad* • Michael Kurinsky
Center Top: *Johnny's mom* • Craig Kellman
Center Middle: *Johnny's mom* • Craig Kellman
Center Bottom & Below: *Johnny's mom* • Stephen DeStefano (designs), Michael Kurinsky (paint)

BELOW: *Johnny's sister • Craig Kellman*
MIDDLE: *Johnny's sister • Stephen DeStefano*
RIGHT: *Johnny's sister • Stephen DeStefano (design), Kristy Kay (paint)*

For Linda's visual inspiration, the team referenced "Martha Stewart, which is evident by her perfectly coiffed mom-bob hairstyle and plain clothes," continues Murdocca.

As for Johnny's dad, Mike, the team first played around with his size. Mike started out as a large, rotund man, but as production continued, he was fashioned into more of a husky, athletic character—the polar opposite of Johnny. Unlike Linda, Mike's personality is understated. For the most part, he is easygoing and more aloof, and he spends a lot of his time apologizing for his wife's comments.

When it came time to design Johnny's siblings, the team decided they wanted them to be more like their parents than their brother. For Johnny's brothers, Kent and Brett, "we wanted them to be chips off the old block, like their father," says Murdocca.

Both brothers are larger than Johnny and have the stature of highschool athletes. "There's a lot of subtext we didn't touch upon in the first movie," concludes Tartakovsky, "but you can really read into it that Johnny wasn't happy living a bland, suburban lifestyle. He didn't fit into the same mold his siblings did—he's the misfit dreamer."

To build Johnny's family, the team was able to use the Johnny model as a starting point. "All of the models created for Johnny's family were based on him—his mother, father, brothers, and sister, which is why they look similar," says animation supervisor Alan Hawkins. This allowed the team to get up and running more quickly than if they had started each from scratch.

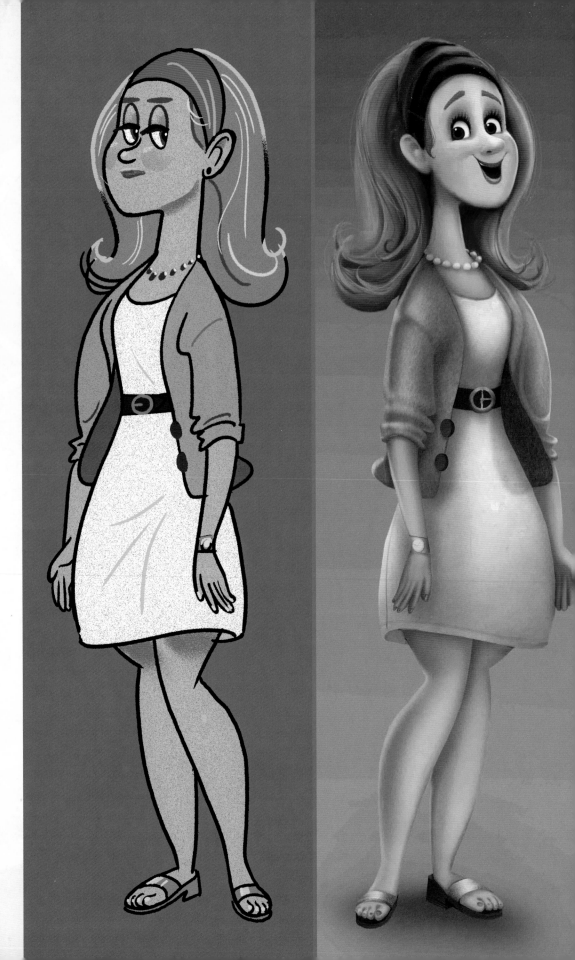

Top Left: *Johnny's brothers • Stephen DeStefano*
Top Right: *Johnny's brothers • Craig Kellman*
Below: *Johnny's three cousins • Tony Siruno*

HAUNTED COUTURE

"It's always about family for Dracula, and that's what makes him such an endearing character. His heart is always in the right place."
— GENNDY TARTAKOVSKY · DIRECTOR

FROM A DESIGN PERSPECTIVE, Dracula and Mavis are visually the same as they appeared in the first movie. However, with Mavis's marriage to Johnny, "Dracula is a little worried that he's going to lose his baby girl," says producer Michelle Murdocca.

Mavis is Dracula's only remaining family, representing his only connection to his deceased wife, Martha. Dracula doesn't want to lose that connection, so he is wary when Johnny proposes marriage. But if marrying a human encourages Drac's "Mavy Wavy" to stay at the hotel and makes her happy, the doting father is prepared to make some concessions.

The most important change to Mavis—or rather to Mavis's wardrobe—is her wedding dress, which the team as a whole was really excited to conceptualize. The task of designing this important asset was placed in the capable hands of artist Seonna Hong. "We wanted a traditional wedding dress—simple and elegant, and something along the lines of what Mavis would really wear. What Seonna came up with tied in perfectly with the vampire-monster theme. It's black, long, has a train, and is pinned up in the back. More importantly, it is a garment that people in the audience will find beautiful in its monstery-ness," says producer Michelle Murdocca.

The *pièce de résistance* of the dress is the spiderweb veil, which pays homage to the scene in the first movie where Johnny painted a picture of the world using spider webs and fireflies to show Mavis what it would be like. "We looked at a lot of gothic attire, and we thought it would be cool to make the veil out of spider webs," says director Genndy Tartakovsky.

"We think it fits perfectly in the monster world," adds Murdocca. "It's definitely part of Mavis's persona—it's sparkly, like golden thread, and is absolutely beautiful."

As a matter of consequence, pulling off the stunning outfit relied heavily on how it was lit. "Since the veil is so detailed, we had to make sure the lighting in the scene hit it just right," explains Murdocca. "We put lights where there normally wouldn't be lights and made sure to achieve the sparkle, shine, and shimmer effect we were going after. We wanted the audience to be able to tell it's a spider web. Otherwise, it could have very easily looked thin and blended in with the rest of the dress."

ABOVE: *Storyboards • Denise Koyama*
RIGHT: *Wedding dress turnarounds • Seonna Hong*

"It was a fun challenge to convey character emotions without words—these kinds of moments are what a story artist lives for!"
— DENISE KOYAMA · STORY ARTIST

"I wanted the dress to look very Beetlejuice-esque, both gothic and youthful—something befitting Winona Ryder's character."
— SEONNA HONG · VISUAL DEVELOPMENT ARTIST

RIGHT: *The Happy Couple portrait • Michael Kurinsky*
BOTTOM: *Flower girl (before & after) • Andre Medina (design), Chin Ko (paint)*
OPPOSITE: *Wedding ceremony • Dean Gordon (paint)*

WEDDING BELLS

THE FIRST MAJOR EVENT of the movie is Johnny and Mavis's wedding—the ceremony where they commit to their "zing" for all eternity. "We wanted the ceremony to be majestic, but we wanted the light to be very soft and beautiful, which is different than the way we normally light our environments," says director Genndy Tartakovsky. "Typically, we have a lot of candlelight, which is rather dark and doesn't quite fill the room like electric lights. I wanted it to feel very dreamy and 'glowy.'"

Production designer Michael Kurinsky and the team began to review various locations of the previously built castle, ultimately deciding to take the pool area from the first movie and transform it into a wonderful backdrop for the wedding. "Since the pool was outside and had a beautiful mountain vista in the distance, we thought it would make the perfect location," says Kurinsky.

After setting up the Chuppa in the altar, draperies made from the same material as Mavis's veil—spider webs—were hung behind it to achieve Tartakovsky's visual goal. The draperies are held up at the corners by bats and, like the veil, are lit by hundreds of fireflies, softly illuminating Johnny and Mavis.

In addition to creating a scene with soft, magical light, "we wanted the colors to be associated with Mavis," adds producer Michelle Murdocca. "If you look at her room in the first movie, there are a lot of pinks and some purple—as opposed to red, which is more evident in the color schemes associated with Dracula."

The job of delivering the exact lighting everyone desired fell on visual effects supervisor Karl Herbst and his team. "For the most part, we already had all the assets for this scene, so the challenge was creating the proper illumination using warm and inviting lighting," he explains.

This became especially challenging when the lighting team turned to the big wedding guest crowd, which is filled with both monsters and humans. "Vampires, for instance, are very pasty-skinned characters, and we tend to light them with warm colors because we want people to make a positive connection to them and not think they're evil," Herbst says. "But when you have a human near a vampire, we had to make the vampire pastier than we would like, so there's some separation between them and the humans. It's a really fine line to walk."

"Dracula would not have hand-picked Johnny to be Mavis's husband, but she loves him, and like any dad, Dracula wants his little girl to be happy."
— MICHELLE MURDOCCA · PRODUCER

"Even though I didn't design the first movie, I had this great set to work with. I like the idea of taking a familiar space and showing it off in a different way."
— MICHAEL KURINSKY · PRODUCTION DESIGNER

BELOW: *Storyboard • John Norton*
RIGHT: *Kelsey • Stephen DeStefano (design), Chin Ko (paint)*

THE BRIDESMAIDS

No wedding, whether for a human or monster, would be complete without a few bridesmaids. In the first movie, so much attention was placed on Johnny and Mavis's budding relationship that audiences never found out if Mavis had any friends. "It was great that we were able to create friends for Mavis, since we didn't see any in the first movie," says production designer Michael Kurinsky.

Adds producer Michelle Murdocca, "We didn't get a chance to create too many unique monsters because we already had a big library of characters from which to choose. Genndy's direction to the team was just to make something that was fun and creepy-looking." And out of the artists' imagination, Kelsey and Clarabelle were born.

Kelsey is described as "a monster valley girl," according to director Genndy Tartakovsky. To help guide her design, Kurinsky asked the artists to "make her ocean based." Kelsey's final design includes tentacles and octopus-like legs. Even the hair on top of her head is fashioned like coral.

For Clarabelle, Tartakovsky wanted a character that looked like a troll that had emerged from some dark, primordial forest. "For me, the comedy comes when you see these two insanely ugly creatures in classy, satin dresses," says Kurinsky.

"It's hard to put ugly on ugly, but we managed that with these two."
— GENNDY TARTAKOVSKY
· DIRECTOR

JOHNNY'S BROTHER ESCORTS BRIDESMAIDE KELSEY DOWN ISLE

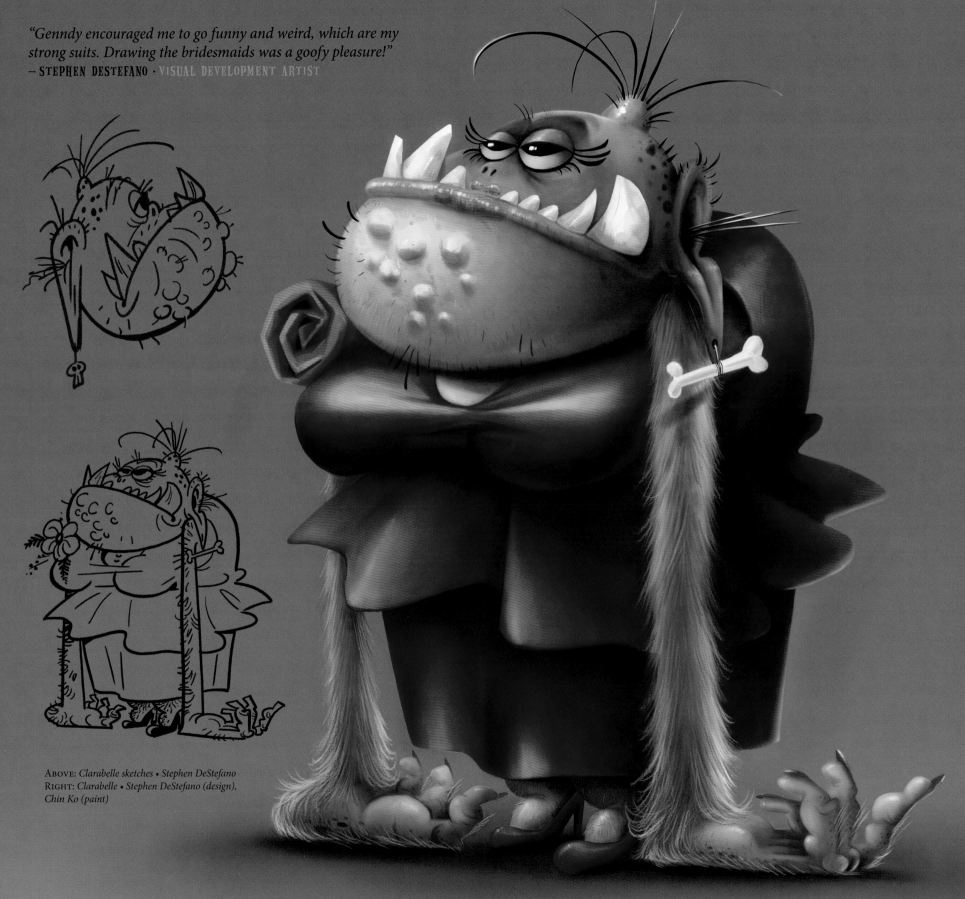

"Genndy encouraged me to go funny and weird, which are my strong suits. Drawing the bridesmaids was a goofy pleasure!"
— STEPHEN DESTEFANO · VISUAL DEVELOPMENT ARTIST

ABOVE: *Clarabelle sketches* • Stephen DeStefano
RIGHT: *Clarabelle* • Stephen DeStefano (design),
Chin Ko (paint)

THIS PAGE (CLOCKWISE):
Formal wear poses: Wayne, Wanda, Murray, Frank, Eunice • Tony Siruno (costume design), Seonna Hong (paint)

ABOVE LEFT: *The Invisible Man (formal wear) • Seonna Hong (paint)*
ABOVE: *Blobby (formal wear) • Seonna Hong (paint)*
LEFT: *Storyboards • John Norton*

THE GHOST LIST

F OR THE WEDDING, it was important to populate the scene with as many guests as possible, which included monsters and humans alike. Fortunately for the team, they already had a gallery of ghouls ready and waiting in their digital repository. "It basically amounted to all the monster creatures we saw in the first movie, including all of Dracula's monster friends, as well as a host of gargoyles, gillmen, gremlins, witches, and more," says director Genndy Tartakovsky.

The character models didn't need much, if any, modifications, but the returning monsters do sport new costumes, with Dracula's close friends having received more attention than other characters. "The formal wear for the gang is very befitting of each one of their personalities," explains production designer Michael Kurinsky. "Murray's attire is very hip, which certainly fits his character. Wayne's tux is definitely a throwback to the 1970s, and it seems like he's had it forever. Wayne is also the only character in the party who is wearing a color other than black, white, or deep magenta."

For Eunice, the team experimented with various lengths and patterns for her dress, the thought being that it needed to be bold and loud, just like her. After exploring many options, the decision was made to go with a black-and-white cheetah pattern.

Perhaps the most unique formal wear of all is "worn" by Blobby. Kurinsky gave the artists two directions to explore for Blobby's attire: put Blobby in a tux or put a tux in Blobby. Ultimately, the team made the decision to have the tux inside of Blobby. "That became the joke. There was no question. Of course he absorbs the tux!" says Kurinsky.

"Even though Dracula's accepted humans into his hotel, he's still tentative about the whole thing. Dracula finds it hard to accept change."
— GENNDY TARTAKOVSKY · DIRECTOR

"The fun for me is seeing how Johnny's parents react to the family of vampires their son is marrying into. It makes for good comedy."
— DAVID WACHTENHEIM · HEAD OF STORY

"Henry's really just a big, loving teddy bear that wants to go around hugging everybody. He doesn't realize that he is actually hurting people."
— MICHAEL KURINSKY · PRODUCTION DESIGNER

OPPOSITE TOP *Storyboards* · *Michael Smukavic*
OPPOSITE BOTTOM: *Film frame*
RIGHT: *Henry* · *Stephen DeStefano (design),*
Michael Kurinsky (paint)

LEFT: *Hotel lobby • Michael Kurinsky (paint)*
BELOW: *Extended family storyboard • Michael Smukavic*

THE WEDDING RECEPTION

T O SET THE STAGE for the party after the ceremony, the team completely transformed the hotel lobby seen in the first movie. "We wanted to soften up the lobby for the reception. It's an old, very cold castle with a lot of stone. We wanted to really warm it up and make it feel more feminine, more inviting," explains director Genndy Tartakovsky.

The rose-colored lighting in the reception scene was meant to make the room feel welcoming for both monsters and humans alike. "It's not monstrous or wacky at all; it's monster formal and themed with Mavis in mind," says production designer Michael Kurinsky.

One of the most unique items in the reception is the wedding cake, which is reminiscent of the scream cheese seen in the first movie. Like the cheese, the cake has been monsterfied and comes alive when touched. "As the cake is being cut and the pieces are removed, the cake cries out," says Tartakovsky.

"To enhance the warm and inviting palette, the guest attire for this sequence was a little richer—the bridesmaids, even the shrunken head, wore rose-colored dresses!"
— STEVE LUMLEYN · ART DIRECTOR

ABOVE: *Johnny (formal wear)* • *Seonna Hong*
MIDDLE: *Fly-trap centerpieces* • *Michael Kurinsky*
RIGHT: *Dracula (formal wear)* • *Seonna Hong*
BOTTOM: *Ballroom/wedding reception* • *Michael Kurinsky*

"*The cake is a monster and the plant centerpieces are alive. It's really fun for kids and adults who watch the movie—we didn't want it to look like a real wedding reception.*"
— GENNDY TARTAKOVSKY · DIRECTOR

MAVIS and JOHNNY CUT THEIR WEDDING CAKE.

ABOVE: Storyboard • John Norton
LEFT: Wedding cake • Stephen DeStefano
(design), Chin Ko (paint)

THINGS THAT GO BUMP!

Adding to the Dracula bloodline is a big deal, so the team got together to devise an appropriate plan for the reveal. "Initially, we went from the wedding right into the birth of the baby," says director Genndy Tartakovksy. But rather than rush into it, Genndy and crew decided they wanted to slow down just a bit so as not to let such an important story point go to waste.

"We wanted to have a moment where Mavis reveals to Dracula that she's pregnant. It's an important, intimate event for both the daughter and father, so we constructed a scene where they go on a 'fly' together, which is essentially the same thing as humans going for a walk," explains Tartakovsky.

"It was actually an idea we pulled from the first movie. We had a scene with Martha and Dracula where she tells him she's pregnant with Mavis," adds producer Michelle Murdocca.

The scene also gave the team a chance to show Dracula and Mavis together away from the castle. "It was hard to find moments where we could get a glimpse inside Dracula and Mavis's relationship—quiet, soft moments with just the two of them. This was a way to do so, where we're not in another room at the hotel, but out in an environment where they used to go flying all the time. It really is a sweet moment," says Murdocca.

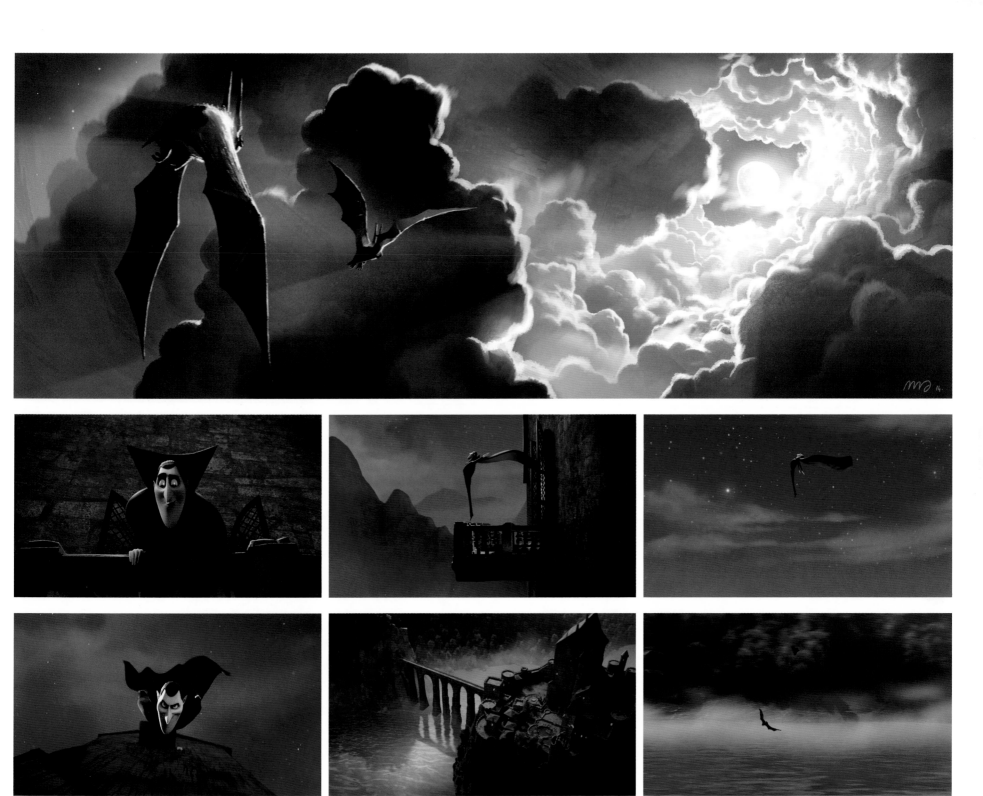

FAR LEFT: *Lighting key • Michael Kurinsky*
LEFT: *Storyboards • Denise Koyama*
TOP: *Transylvanian clouds • Sylvain Marc*
ABOVE: *Lighting keys • Michael Kurinsky*

"Mavis wants to reveal she's pregnant in a unique way, as only vampires can, while playing a game with her father, Dracula."
— DENISE KOYAMA · STORY ARTIST

"Silhouette value is really important to me. When we worked on the scene where Mavis reveals she's pregnant, there was a lot of work to get her to look charming and cute as a bat with a little baby bump."
— GENNDY TARTAKOVSKY · DIRECTOR

FLIGHT NIGHT!

Bringing the pregnancy reveal to flight onscreen was no small feat, as the team had to balance cartoon-like environments and realistic elements. "The challenge," explains director Genndy Tartakovsky, "was to make the scene feel real without making it look one-hundred-percent real."

The team also faced an additional challenge: The scene takes place at night; a necessity in a movie dealing with vampires. There was a worry that it would be a little too dark and depressing. The first task, then, was to ensure there was ample lighting, which was accomplished by tactfully using moonlight to create a naturally lit setting.

Next, visual effects supervisor Karl Herbst and his team created cloud cover. During the rough layout and animation phase, Herbst chose to use proxy geometry for the foreground clouds since it was easier and faster than visualizing volumes. This helped established depth and speed for both camera motion and the flight of the bats.

From there, the animation team was able to make some of the shapes transparent so the characters would be visible as they flew through the cloud proxies. Once animation was complete, Herbst's team updated the lay-out of clouds in the effects department with the true volumes and expanded the clouds to the density needed for the final look. "We normally try to have our pipeline work in a linear fashion: layout, animation, effects, and then simulation. But when working with volume rendering, we found the looping between effects and lighting was the most efficient way to get the look we needed," says Herbst.

To achieve the desired result, the visual effects team reshaped the clouds to look more like stacks of cotton balls. It was then just a matter of finding the right balance of small and large clouds, and adding a fluffy layer to blend them together to create the final look.

Top : *Cloud color study • Miguel Gil*
Left : *Cloud color study • Sylvain Marc (design), Miguel Gil (paint)*
Above & Right: *Cloud studies • Sylvain Marc*

"The design combines elements of both the human and monster worlds, which creates an excellent contrast."
— JOEY CHOU · VISUAL DEVELOPMENT ARTIST

THE SWEET SUITE

WHEN IT CAME TO LIVING QUARTERS, there was really no question where Mavis and Johnny would live—it was just a matter of working out the details. "We essentially revamped Mavis's old bedroom and made it into a master suite," recalls production designer Michael Kurinsky. The area is diamond-shaped, containing a central parlor room for entertaining guests with two bedrooms off to either side.

For the décor, it was important to strike a balance between the monstrous and the human. "At first we had a lot of Johnny's travel posters everywhere, but it didn't feel right. We also felt that the couple would need a space that looked more grown up, since they would be recently married and about to become parents," says director Genndy Tartakovsky.

The interior set dressing reflects both Mavis and Johnny. Instead of posters, a Hawaiian hat and a big Tiki mask hang on the walls. On the shelves are photographs of the couple's trip around the world, along with little knickknacks they picked up. The furniture resembles what you might find in a gothic version of Pottery Barn.

BELOW: *Furniture and props • Michael Kurinsky (design)*
BOTTOM: *Hotel suite interior • Joey Chou (paint)*
TOP OPPOSITE: *Lighting key • Chin Ko*

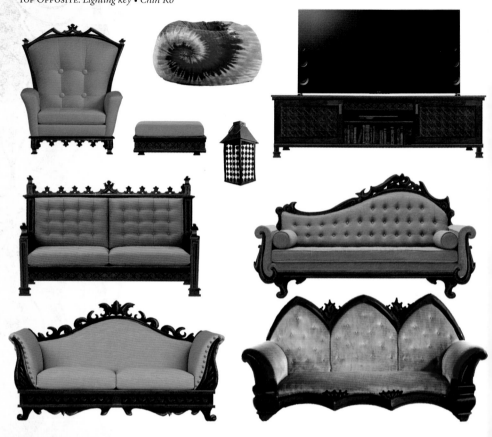

BOTTOM LEFT: *Hospital corridor • Chin Ko*
BELOW RIGHT: *Storyboards • John Norton*
OPPOSITE TOP LEFT: *Face to face • Chin Ko*
OPPOSITE TOP RIGHT: *The happy family • Miguel Gil*
OPPOSITE: *Hospital room • Miguel Gil*

NURSE...DRACULA?

WHEN IT CAME TIME to birth the delivery room look, the production team's first idea was to create a straightforward hospital that catered to humans and monsters alike. But according to production designer Michael Kurinsky, "It felt odd. Even though humans now accept monsters, it just didn't feel right."

Instead, the decision was made to create a space specifically for monsters. "We weren't deliberately trying to make the room feel like it was part of the castle, or that it could even be part of the castle. We just wanted something that felt very grounded in the monster world," says Kurinsky.

For the employees of the ghoulish delivery room, the team reached back into their monster-character toy box and pulled out a few fetid gems for the doctor, nurse, and orderlies. "Our doctor is based on the Dr. Jekyll character from the first movie," explains director Genndy Tartakovsky. "We tweaked him a bit by dressing him in doctor's scrubs and giving him fangs. Our nurse is one of our ugly witch-hags, and our orderlies are zombies."

To top it all off, there's a scene where Dracula dresses in drag to infiltrate the delivery room. "It's a classic gag that is traced all the way back to the Three Stooges and the Marx Brothers," says Tartakovsky. "He basically hypnotizes one of the nurses and puts on her uniform. It doesn't quite fit, so he has to put pillows over the top of his backside and stuff his shirt with balloons."

"Dracula dressed as a nurse in a wig is so silly, but you still feel the excitement radiating from him as he sees Dennis for the first time."

— CHIN KO · VISUAL DEVELOPMENT ARTIST

DENISOVICH

Dennis, the grandson of the world's most famous vampire, looks decidedly human, which is of great concern to Dracula. Rather than sporting raven-colored hair and bearing sharp fangs, Dennis appears to take after his human lineage. "We wanted Dennis to look like a combination of Johnny and Mavis," says director Genndy Tartakovsky, "but we wanted Johnny's traits to come through a bit more, so he looks more human and goofy. Dracula still loves him, but he certainly wonders why his own strong vampire genes aren't dominant in Dennis's features."

From the first moment Dennis is onscreen, his red hair immediately defines him. In fact, he comes into the world with one giant red curl on top of his head. As Dennis gets older, the hair becomes more pronounced.

"When character designer Craig Kellman gave us his first designs, Dennis had this incredible crop of hair," says production designer Michael Kurinsky. "One of the hardest things I had to do during the project was accurately paint a rendering of the hair and pass it on to Imageworks so they could create the model. What they came up with was nothing short of amazing."

"At times, we're able to make things seem so real that it clashes with the cartoon style we're ultimately going for. It starts to feel odd when you have cartoony characters in a photo-real environment."
— GENNDY TARTAKOVSKY ·
DIRECTOR

"Dracula and Dennis have a very sweet, playful relationship; Dennis really does love his Vampa."
— MICHELLE MURDOCCA · PRODUCER

This Spread: *Dennis* • *Craig Kellman*

Top Far Left: *Dennis in PJs* • Seonna Hong *(paint)*
Bottom Far Left: *Dennis Batman* • Chin Ko
Left: *Dennis Dracula* • Michael Kurinsky *(design)*, Seonna Hong
(costume and hair design)
Right: *Dennis* • Michael Kurinsky

BIG HAIR!

One of the most important characters in *Hotel Transylvania 2* is not a monster or a human, but rather Dennis's curly locks of hair! To say the job of making his red mane come to life was a painstaking process would be an extreme understatement.

When character designer Craig Kellman provided the first designs of Dennis to the team, he always drew him with extreme amounts of red hair—to the point that the character designs couldn't simply be handed off to the team at Imageworks. Before that could happen, production designer Michael Kurinsky took on the arduous task of interpreting Kellman's squiggles to create a meticulous rendering of what the hair should look like on screen. "I started thinking of each curl as a cylinder, and then I began painting in shapes that looked cylindrical. Some were pointed directly at the camera, some were on their sides, and some were tilted three-quarters. When I had a design of cylinders that looked right to me, I started making the final touches and adding detail," recalls Kurinsky.

Since lighting is a big consideration in every scene, Kurinsky also had to make sure his rendering accurately portrayed the shades of red the curls would be if they were lit in a bright setting or a dark setting. Once he was confident the rendering would provide Imageworks with solid direction, Kurinsky sent it over.

From there, the Imageworks team went to work. "One of the biggest challenges in creating Dennis's curls was to match the look and feel of the artwork while not making things overly complicated," recalls hair lead Brian Casper. "We started with a single curled strand of hair and then slowly built on top of that by adding different features like wave and rotation."

Once the team had a base curl they liked, they were able to copy it over and over again until Dennis had a full head of hair. When they finished "grooming" Dennis, his model had more than 265 individual strands. Once the computer filled in the rest, there was a grand total of 150,000 hairs!

"Composing Dennis and Dracula in the same shot was a challenge, and at times we only include the top of Dennis's head."
— JAMES WILLIAMS ·
LAYOUT ARTIST

DENNIS'S BEDROOM

FORTUNATELY FOR JOHNNY AND MAVIS, the suite they occupy in the hotel is big enough to accommodate Dennis as well. With a second bedroom off their central parlor, the design team simply needed to redecorate. "We wanted it to be more of a human-looking space," explains director Genndy Tartakovsky. "Mavis is very accepting of who Dennis is and whoever he will become, whether it's monster or human, much like with Johnny. In her mind, Dennis is perfect just as he is."

While the idea was to adorn Dennis's room with more human trappings, it was impossible to completely ignore the duality of his life. The basic structure of his room speaks to his monster side—it's part of an old castle in Transylvania with wood floors and stone walls. What makes it human, then, are its trappings.

"Colorful curtains certainly helped," explains production designer Michael Kurinsky. "But the team was completely unified in adding a racecar bed to make the room really stand out." To really put a human stamp on the space, there is also a Gymboree-style mural on the back wall. But it's not smooth; the relief of the old castle wall come through. "That back wall says it all to me," says Kurinsky. "It's big and monstery, but with the cutest happy sun on it. That's Dennis. He's a kid stuck in between two worlds."

"Dracula is so out of touch with the world around him— it's great to watch him wrap his head around normal, everyday things."
— HENRY YU ·
STORY ARTIST

ABOVE: *Storyboards* • *Henry Yu*
BELOW: *Bedroom mural* • *Joey Chou*
BOTTOM LEFT: *Toys* • *Joey Chou*

TOP RIGHT: *Dennis' room sketch* • *Michael Spooner*
BOTTOM RIGHT: *Dennis' room* • *Joey Chou*

MONSTROUS PROPS

HANG IN THERE BABY

CREATING A MOVIE that combines monster and human motifs provided ample opportunities to build some unique set dressing and props. For Dennis's room, the team was able to get especially creative, reaching into their collective unconscious to come up with accessories that reflect Dennis's eclectic world.

Tailored to Dennis's human side, there's a Mexican wrestling action figure—a gift from his human grandparents. To add monster flair to his collection, there's the ever-popular "My First Guillotine," which is a favorite among monster kids. Even though it's designed with basic wood shapes and bright primary colors, it's incredibly dangerous—if the user isn't careful, they could lose a finger! Then again, that's all part of the monster-y fun!

Top: *Fang measurer • Michael Spooner*
Right: *Doll • Kristy Kay*
Far Right: *Calender • Joey Chou*

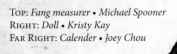

"For the monster baby calendar, we made it much darker-looking than a human baby calendar, while still retaining a sweet, innocent look."
— JOEY CHOU · VISUAL DEVELOPMENT ARTIST

SUN	MON	TUE	WED	THUR	FRI	SAT
1	2	3	4	5	6	7
8	9	10	11	12	13	14
15	16	17	18	19	20	21
22	23	24	25	26	27	28
29	30	31				

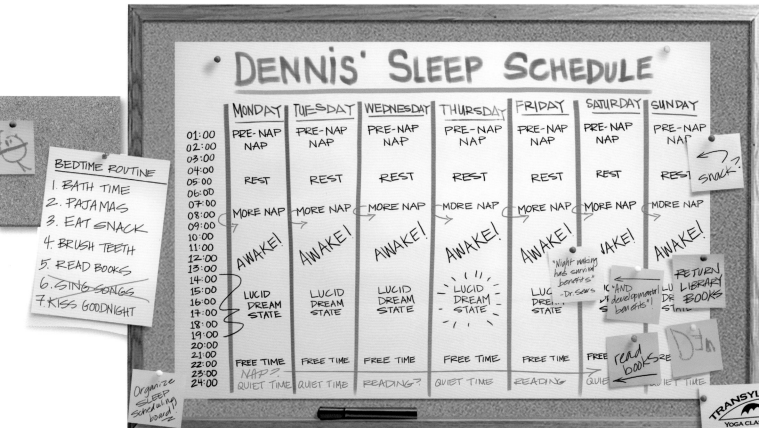

Above: *Sleep schedule baord and notes • Seonna Hong*
Bottom Left: *My First Guillotine box and toy • Michael Kurinsky*

Below: *Wrestler action figure • Seonna Hong*
Bottom Right: *First birthday cake • Joey Chou*

JUST LIKE THE REAL THING BECAUSE IT IS !

MY FIRST GUILLOTINE ™ is an educational toy that will have your little monster chopping heads like a professional executioner in no time.

The lunette will accommodate most body parts as well as small pets.

Parents should heed extreme caution to keep the blade nice and sharp so that their little one won't miss a minute of head choppin' fun !

The lead based paint and stainless steel blade comes clean with just the wipe of a damp cloth.

BELOW: *Kakie Whip can • Todd Gibbs*
BOTTOM: *Kakie set on TV • Joey Chou*
RIGHT TOP: *Kakie • Lizzie Nichols*
RIGHT BOTTOM: *Wuzzlelumpelbum • Chin Ko*

DENNIS'S FAVORITE MONSTERS

"WHEN DRACULA REALIZES that Dennis loves monsters and watches monster shows, he's really excited," says director Genndy Tartakovsky. But Kakie the cake monster and his sidekick Wuzzelumpelbum, Dennis's TV idols, reflect the monster world about as well as Elmo or Cookie Monster do the human world. Quite frankly, it's "insulting to Dracula because they're not real monsters," concludes Tartakovsky.

Kakie and Wuzzelumpelbum's character rigs were designed to resemble those of real puppets and the completed versions look like they have fur made out of actual fabric. "We really wanted them to look like something Jim Henson would have made, to the point that you believe someone is actually holding sticks and pulling them around," recalls visual effects supervisor Karl Herbst. Adds Tartakovsky, "When we animate Kakie and Wuzzelumpelbum it looks like there is a real hand inside manipulating them."

FAR LEFT TOP: *Kakie sketch* • *Craig Kellman*
FAR LEFT BOTTOM: *Storyboard* • *John Norton*
LEFT: *Kakie Monster* • *Craig Kellman*

"*I saw the same thing happen to my own sons that is happening to Dennis. One day they're into Barney, and the next day they are into Batman.*"
— ROBERT MARIANETTI · HEAD OF STORY

CAKEY- SLOW DOWN WHIZZLEWIMPLEBUM! THE SCARIEST MONSTER OF ALL IS DIABETES!

LEFT: *Film frame*
BELOW: *Lighting key • Michael Kurinsky*
TOP RIGHT: *Tennis court model and schematic • Steve Lumley*
MIDDLE RIGHT: *Tennis courts • Aurélien Predal*
BOTTOM RIGHT: *Film frame*

WELCOME ONE AND ALL

W ITH THE WORLD more accepting of monsters, a transformation of sorts has overtaken the hotel. Instead of simply catering to the same ghoulish clientele, Dracula has opened his doors to humans. If that weren't enough, Dracula has also opened his mind to doing things in a new way, even allowing modern human technology to ooze into his frightening manor. "The human element has been pushed further in this movie than in the first," explains director Genndy Tartakovsky. "Dracula really wants to ensure that Johnny and Mavis don't leave the hotel."

Looking at the hotel as a whole, it's pretty much the same as it was in the first movie. To make scenes feel different, the team took the already wonderful set and adjusted the lighting. "You can change the environment and make it look entirely different by just altering the lighting," explains production designer Michael Kurinsky.

When entering the main lobby, it's easy to see a transformation has occurred in order to make it more inviting to the humans who now patronize the hotel. Wherever you look, modern technology has found its place in the monster world, largely thanks to Johnny's influence. "The only thing that's really changed in the hotel from the first movie is it's peppered with modern amenities. The lobby has flat-screen televisions and monitors that display all the activities guests can indulge in while staying at the hotel," explains producer Michelle Murdocca.

"Dracula is like a caveman who just thawed out in the twenty-first century—he has a hard time understanding modern technology."
— HENRY YU • STORY ARTIST

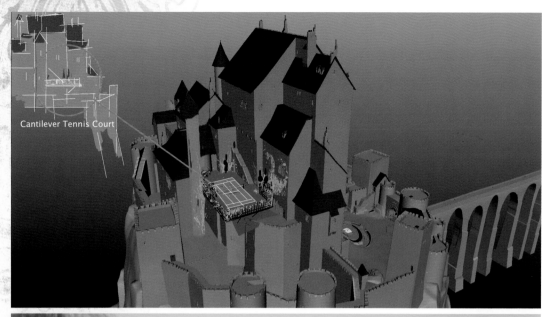

Cantilever Tennis Court

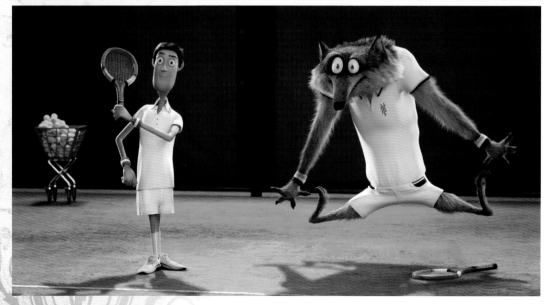

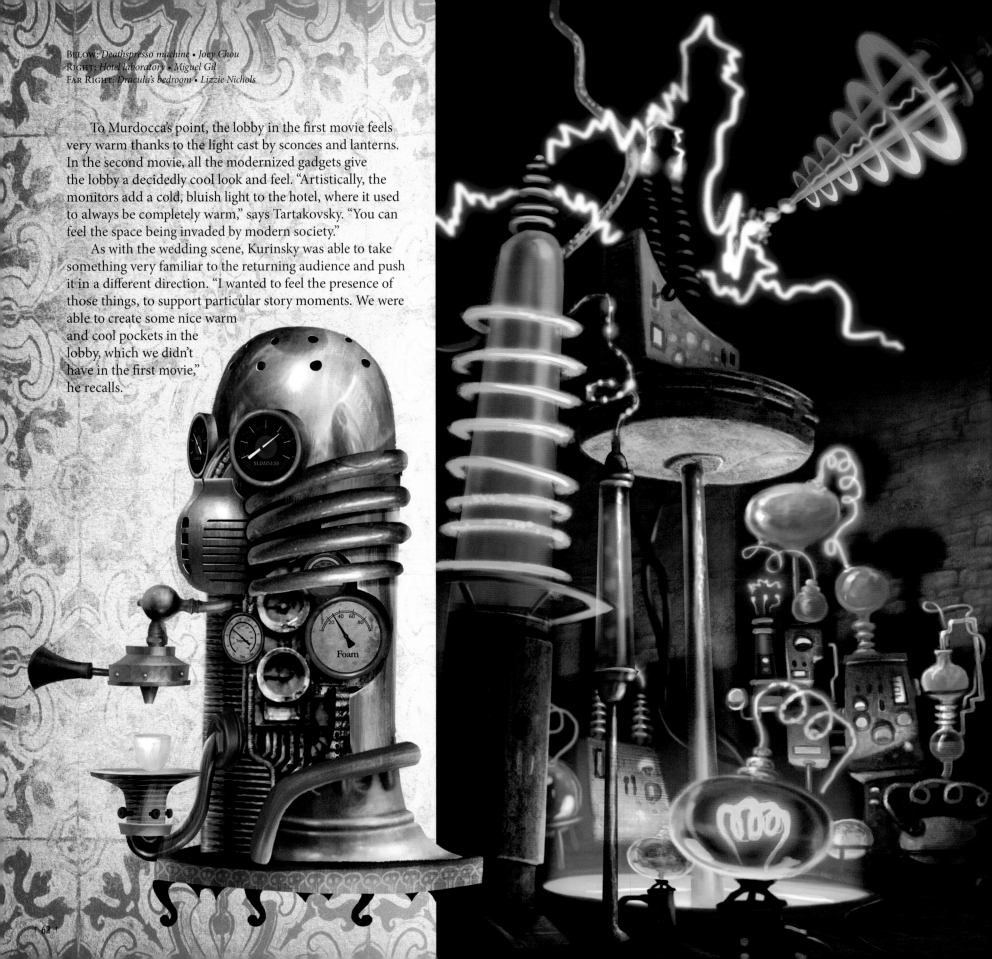

BELOW: *Deathspresso machine* • *Joey Chou*
RIGHT: *Hotel laboratory* • *Miguel Gil*
FAR RIGHT: *Dracula's bedroom* • *Lizzie Nichols*

To Murdocca's point, the lobby in the first movie feels very warm thanks to the light cast by sconces and lanterns. In the second movie, all the modernized gadgets give the lobby a decidedly cool look and feel. "Artistically, the monitors add a cold, bluish light to the hotel, where it used to always be completely warm," says Tartakovsky. "You can feel the space being invaded by modern society."

As with the wedding scene, Kurinsky was able to take something very familiar to the returning audience and push it in a different direction. "I wanted to feel the presence of those things, to support particular story moments. We were able to create some nice warm and cool pockets in the lobby, which we didn't have in the first movie," he recalls.

BELOW: *Porridge Head social media page • Joey Chou*
RIGHT: *Bellhop zombie • Stephen DeStefano (design), Michael Kurinsky (paint)*

FIENDISH ADDITIONS

"**D**RACULA IS LIKE ALL OLD-TIMERS when they first get a new computer: whenever they hear a term like 'jpeg,' they don't know what you're talking about. For instance, most people know what you mean when you say 'Bluetooth.' But to Dracula, Blue Tooth is a little monster that lives in the hotel," explains production designer Michael Kurinsky. Some of the other new employees were created specifically to serve as sources of additional technology-based humor, including a monster that uses a cellphone app to distort his already grotesque visage.

However, two particularly interesting-looking employees were created to reinforce the idea that some activities at the hotel still cater to the standard monster crowd—Harry the Three-Eyed Magician and his "lovely" assistant. Harry's magic-show lounge act, much like the bingo scene in the first movie, is meant to demonstrate that Dracula still has an affinity for archaic forms of monstrous hotel entertainment. "The tricks Harry performs are tailored to the amusement of the monsters in the crowd and are very off-putting and disturbing to the human guests," explains Tartakovsky.

"It's great we get to make jokes based on things that are completely normal for the monster world, but that are a little shocking for humans. That's really what this movie is all about—the shock of the two worlds coming together."
— MICHAEL KURINSKY ·
PRODUCTION DESIGNER

LEFT: *Harry Three-Eye* • *Craig Kellman (design), Seonna Hong (paint)*
MIDDLE: *Blue Tooth* • *Tony Siruno (design), Michael Kurinsky (paint)*
RIGHT: *Harry Three-Eyes's assistant* • *Craig Kellman (design), Seonna Hong (paint)*

*"I loved developing Harry Three-Eyes and his assistant.
When it came to them, the grosser the better!"*
— SEONNA HONG • VISUAL DEVELOPMENT ARTIST

"Creating a brainless zombie wearing ill-fitting clothes to make balloon animals for kids was awesome! Not sure who'd want this guy at their birthday party...."
— ANDRE MEDINA · VISUAL DEVELOPMENT ARTIST

BELOW: *Zombie clown* • *Andre Medina (design),*
Seonna Hong (paint)
TOP RIGHT: *Picnic table* • *Kristy Kay*
BOTTOM RIGHT: *Lanterns* • *Kristy Kay*

"It's a monster party, but with some human influences such as a bouncy house, a zombie clown making balloon animals, a piñata, and a game of limbo."
— GENNDY TARTAKOVSKY · DIRECTOR

Top Left: *Happy Birthday banner • Todd Gibbs*
Below Left: *Ruins • Jim Alles (design)*
Middle Left: *Ruins color • Kristy Kay (paint)*
Bottom Left: *Color key • Aurélien Predal*
Bottom right: *Birthday cake • Todd Gibbs*

WOLF PUPS PARTY

T O CREATE THE BACKDROP for the scene featuring a wolf pup's birthday party, the CG team had to rework the ruins they had originally designed to be viewed from far away and make them higher resolution.

Although the ruins are designed to be reminiscent of those areas in public parks where grass never grows, they feature nice, decorative items. Behind them is an old piece of a long-forgotten castle. "I think it was a great touch that we created the ruins, which was actually a last-minute addition," says production designer Michael Kurinsky.

As for lighting, it needed to be appropriate to the action in the scene. "I wanted the lighting to be very high energy, because the wolf pups are very high energy," explains Kurinsky. "We added some really warm lanterns in the immediate foreground, followed by some atmospheric, cool lighting behind that. So when the action gets big, which it always does with the wolf pups, it is amply supported."

While the set dressing is very human—including lanterns, balloons, and a picnic table—the set combines aesthetics from both the human world and the monster world. The two worlds come together most markedly in the clown that attends the party. "In a way, he's the perfect example of a human and monster hybrid—he has a nice, clean clown suit on, but inside the suit he's a crusty, old zombie," says Kurinsky.

WINNIE

WITH DENNIS DECIDEDLY HUMAN, at least at the beginning of *Hotel Transylvania 2*, there was an opportunity for the team to create a relationship dynamic that echoes Johnny and Mavis's marriage—where human and monster worlds meet—with Dennis's friendship with Winnie, a wolf pup.

"At every turn, the theme of the movie is reinforced: it's about two worlds—monster and human—coming together. If you look at it from Dennis's perspective, he is clearly the one who is the most comfortable with who he is, and it's really everyone around him who is trying to tell him who he is and how the world works. He has no problem being best friends, and possibly more, with Winnie," explains production designer Michael Kurinsky.

To take it even further, Dennis and Winnie's relationship also helps reinforce the concept of the "zing." Even at such an early age, it's clear Dennis and Winnie understand what that means and it manifests itself onscreen in a profound way.

Visually, not too much has changed with Winnie since the first film, although the team did need to re-proportion and upgrade her model since she was basically a clone of one of the male pups, just with a different costume. Not only does she look a bit older, which was achieved by removing her pacifier and altering the look of her fur, but the improved model also features bigger eyes, making her a little cuter. Her rig also received upgrades as well to give it more range.

"Denise and Darrell's boards always inject an incredible amount of humor and energy into their scenes."
— GENNDY TARTAKOVSKY · DIRECTOR

ABOVE: *Storyboards* • *Denise Koyama*
BELOW: *Storyboards* • *Darrell Rooney*

ACT
2

"One of the hardest things to do is design something without much character. While there is certainly some character in the human world—it's not completely devoid— it's definitely a place that isn't as exciting as Transylvania. And that's on purpose."
— STEVE LUMLEY · ART DIRECTOR

"We wanted the human neighborhood to be just diverse enough without creating any individual, eclectic houses. Each one has the look and feel of a tract house."
— MICHAEL KURINSKY · PRODUCTION DESIGNER

LEFT: *California suburbs • Joey Chou*
BOTTOM: *Lighting key • Miguel Gil*
OVERLEAF TOP: *Californian shoreline • Sylvain Marc (design)*
OVERLEAF BOTTOM: *Californian shoreline color • Miguel Gil (paint)*

THE HUMAN WORLD

WHEN IT SEEMS AS IF DENNIS is human rather than monster, Mavis feels it might be better if he spent more time with people who are like he is as he gets older. To test the theory, Johnny and Mavis take a trip to Johnny's hometown of Santa Cruz in order to scope things out. Leaving Dennis in the care of Dracula (who embarks on his own road trip with Dennis—more on that later), Mavis and Johnny head to California to visit his parents. For the first time in a *Hotel Transylvania* movie, the audience gets to see a representation of where humans live.

"One of the first things I designed was this alternate, human world," recalls art director Steve Lumley, "which is a total contrast to the monster world." The design direction was to make it look like a boring place. As opposed to the vertical structures, dynamic lighting, and saturated colors of the monster world, the human world is characterized by horizontal structures, flat lighting, and bland colors. "Essentially, I designed three or four modular pieces that could be arranged into any house that we needed. I literally turned off my creative side and just built square and rectangular boxes of various shapes and sizes," he concludes.

Overall, everything in the human world blends in together, which was the goal. While there is a little bit of color to the human world, everything is fairly neutral when compared to the hotel.

The one exception is a shot of the California coast, which Mavis and Johnny drive along as they make their way to his parents' house. The team wanted to make it "pretty and not totally bland," explains production designer Michael Kurinsky, "because it was the only opportunity to show the California coast in all its wonderful, beautiful glory. Everything else in the human world is very average, so we wanted to create this special moment."

To get around the issue of Mavis's aversion to direct sunlight, the team "magically kept her in a position where she is always in shadow," explains visual effects supervisor Karl Herbst, "so we could give the scene the sense that it's the 'golden hour.'"

THE MINI MART

BEFORE ARRIVING at her in-laws' house, Mavis is captivated by a mini mart she spots along the road, and she excitedly demands that Johnny stop so they can go inside. The overall design of the mart follows the same aesthetics as the rest of the structures in the human world: it's a flat, horizontal, single-story building. The team broke convention, however, by plussing up the visuals just a bit. "We wanted to make the ordinary extraordinary, and this was the one place in the human world where we could feature a lot of color," explains production designer Michael Kurinsky. "Even though Mavis comes from a world that is full of color and fantastic things, the mini mart pops out at her—in her mind it's like an amusement park."

Once inside, Mavis's enthusiasm hits a zenith when she sees a slushy machine. This is where the team really pushed the use of color. "We really wanted to draw attention to it, so we used rainbow-bright colors. It's the most colorful thing we see in the human world," recalls Kurinsky. "Mavis is simply a tourist who finds something that humans see every day extraordinary and fantastic. If you pay attention to the human characters in the lobby of the hotel, you will notice that they take photographs of almost everything around them, because they too find something extraordinary in the things monsters would deem ordinary and commonplace."

BELOW: *Cashier face studies • Tony Siruno*
BOTTOM: *Film frame*
RIGHT: *Kal • Todd Gibbs*
OPPOSITE TOP: *Mini mart interior • Jim Alles (design)*
OPPOSITE BOTTOM: *Slushy machines • Chin Ko (paint)*

KAL

K AL IS THE MINI MART ATTENDANT who completely personifies a human in the human world. Nothing fazes him, nothing excites him, and nothing, not even Mavis' over-exuberance regarding the world around him, can break Kal out of his stupor. To him, the slushy machine and vast selection of potato chips are no big deal. Kal's appearance perfectly complements his demeanor thanks to a uniform that conforms to the human world's color palette. His drab-looking skin and deep, sunken eyes complete Kal's nonplussed expression. Even in his brief interaction with Mavis, Kal never breaks character, even though she is clearly excited by everything around her in the mini mart. To him, it's all very commonplace and bland.

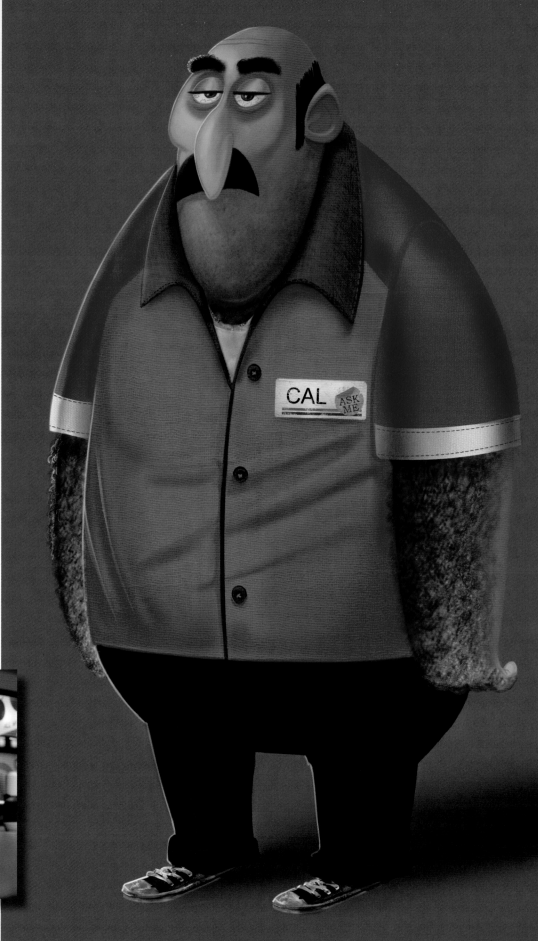

"*To Mavis, the mini mart is new and exciting, but to humans it's standard and bland, bordering on invisible.*"
— MICHAEL KURINSKY · PRODUCTION DESIGNER

WALL MOUNTED
PEGBOARD PANEL

ATM
MACHINE

OPEN
ALL NIGHT

PLAY
lottery
HERE

99¢ HOT DOGS 99¢

HOT
DOG
COOKER

3 WALL SHELF UNITS WITH GENERIC PRODUCTS

Strawberry   GREEN APPLE   +vitamin C Blueberry   CHERRY SODA   WATERMELON

MANGO   Bubble Gum   BLUE RASPBERRY   organic BERRY 100% $1.99 TROPICAL ORANGE

grape grape grape   COLA   ALL NATURAL APPLE   Dark Chocolate   Banana

THE SKATE PARK

THE SKATE PARK is another location in the human world that is visually uninspiring and unappealing—that is, until Mavis arrives. At first the production team thought they would make the park really dynamic with brightly lit signs. Ultimately, though, it was decided that the park needed to follow the same conventions as the rest of the human world, making it bland and uninteresting.

All it took was Mavis to make things pop. "Like the mini mart, Mavis brings the excitement to the park," says production designer Michael Kurinsky. "She energizes the world with color and light after jumping on the bike to take it for a spin."

While showing off her arsenal of vampiric BMX skills, Mavis reaches heights no human can achieve as she proceeds to ride along the power lines high above the park. During her magnificent display, sparks shoot everywhere in a fantastic spectacle. Once again, Mavis finds a way to infuse monster-sized life into an otherwise unremarkable setting.

LEFT: *Skate park* • Miguel Gil
BOTTOM LEFT: *Storyboards* • Graham Keith Baxter
ABOVE RIGHT: *Film frame*

"The idea of adding power lines for Mavis to ride on opened up all kinds of possibilities, which the animators and visual effects teams took full advantage of."
— GRAHAM KEITH BAXTER • STORY ARTIST

BELOW: *Neighborhood houses* • *Steve Lumley*
RIGHT TOP, MIDDLE AND OPPOSITE TOP: *Parents' house* • *Joey Chou*
RIGHT BOTTOM: *Neighborhood schematic* • *Steve Lumley*
OPPOSITE BOTTOM: *Parents' house and backyard* • *Steve Lumley*

SUBURBAN LIFE

W HEN THE PRODUCTION TEAM first started discussing how Johnny's parents' house would look, their first impulse was to make it an eccentric-looking home— something with a little character to it. But once the team took a step back, they realized they needed the house to serve the movie's goal of contrasting the human and monster worlds by offering a visual counterpoint to monster home life.

Art director Steve Lumley created a modern home for Mike and Linda made completely out of squares, finishing it off with a tan, off-white color to make it as drab and boring as possible. "So when Mavis walks in, she's basically a black silhouette that doesn't stand out," says production designer Michael Kurinsky.

Conversely, Linda, the mother, is dressed in white and khaki, and Mike, the dad, is dressed in shades of brown, so neither one of them stands out either. The only character who does stand out is Johnny with his colorful clothing.

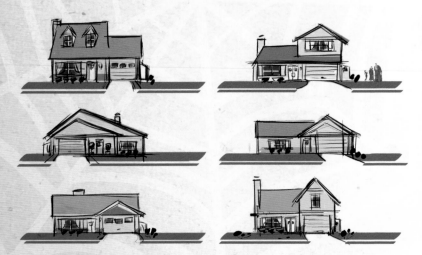

"*The challenge of creating the human world was it needed to completely contrast with the more dramatic monster world.*"
— STEVE LUMLEY • ART DIRECTOR

"*In the monster world, we have spotlights. But in the human world, the lighting is very even. Every corner is accounted for and everything is overexposed.*"
— MICHAEL KURINSKY • PRODUCTION DESIGNER

"When you get inside the parents' house, the lighting is much like for a sitcom. The whole scene appears very flat."
— KARL HERBST ·
VISUAL EFFECTS DIRECTOR

ABOVE & BELOW: *Living room • Joey Chou*
OPPOSITE TOP: *Kitchen • Steve Lumley (design),*
Chin Ko (paint)
OPPOSITE BOTTOM: *Living room •*
Steve Lumley (design), Chin Ko (paint)

JOHNNY'S BEDROOM

A s JOHNNY AND MAVIS enter Johnny's old bedroom, the room where they will stay while visiting his parents, they are treated to quite a spectacle. In an effort to make Mavis feel more at "home," Linda has transformed half the room into a display reminiscent of a seasonal Halloween party store, complete with pumpkin-themed lights, bats on wires hanging from the ceiling, and a tombstone emblazoned with the acronym "R.I.P." Unfortunately, Linda wasn't able to procure a proper coffin for Mavis to sleep in, so she substituted the utility box from the pool shed.

While the bedroom is only glimpsed briefly, the set cleaves to the film's consistent use of color. Mavis's side of the room is very bright, both because Johnny's parents think that's how a monster's room should look and because it reflects the Transylvanian color palette. Even though there is a bit of color on Johnny's side of the room, it's not enough to overpower the sense of how bland everything in the human world really is.

"The way we ended up designing the room, it's almost like a perfect split down the middle. You can almost see the line where one side falls off and the other takes over."
— MICHAEL KURINSKY · PRODUCTION DESIGNER

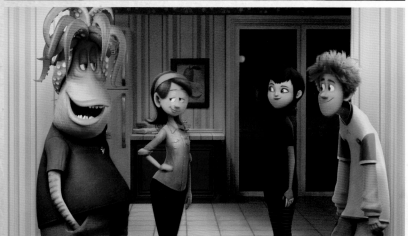

OPPOSITE LEFT: *Lighting keys* • *Chin Ko*
LEFT: *Pandragora* • *Andre Medina (design), Seonna Hong (paint)*
BELOW: *Paul sketch* • *Andre Medina (design)*
RIGHT: *Paul* • *Joey Chou (paint)*

THE NEIGHBORS

As it turns out, monsters don't just live in Transylvania. They also live in California. Well, sort of. As a way of showing she's trying to be tolerant and accepting of her new daughter-in-law, Linda decides to invite over two couples that she thinks are mixed monster couples like Johnny and Mavis. This is her way of telling Johnny and Mavis that if they decide to move to California, they won't feel out of place as the only human-monster couple in the neighborhood.

The first couple to arrive is Pandragora and Caren. Pandragora is a laidback sea creature–like monster with living, dreadlock-like tentacles for hair and webbed hands. While the colors picked for his navy-green shirt and khaki shorts are fairly neutral (so he blends in more easily with his human surroundings), he's colorful by nature.

The other couple is Loretta and Paul. Linda mistakenly thinks Paul is a werewolf, but he is really just an exceptionally hairy man with long hair and a thick beard.

"Paul's not a werewolf, but rather a cool, laid-back, and extremely hairy hipster. I mean that's a beard to be envied."
— ANDRE MEDINA •
VISUAL DEVELOPMENT ARTIST

† 89 †

ROAD TRIP!

WHILE JOHNNY AND MAVIS are in Santa Cruz, Dracula orchestrates a little road trip to all his favorite old monster haunts in order to try and coax Dennis into becoming a vampire. "Dracula thinks that if he can get Dennis away for just a little bit and show him some real old-school monstery stuff, it will get Dennis's fangs to come out," says production designer Michael Kurinsky.

Dennis has yet to show any signs of fangs (what is referred to in the vampire world as a "late fanger"), which has Dracula concerned that Dennis may be completely human after all. Moreover, Mavis has been overprotective with Dennis, exposing him primarily to "monsters" that aren't really monsters, encouraging un-monster-like behavior such as sharing with others, and feeding him human foods like avocados instead of monster-appropriate delicacies such as mice.

Before animating could begin, the hearse needed to be updated and all of Dracula's monster friends who go along for the ride needed to be modified so they would fit inside. The team simply pushed the curtain behind the front seat back a bit, and then added two extra rows: one for Murray and Wayne, and one for Frank.

Simply adjusting the vehicle wasn't enough, though, so the animators came up with some great compositions that made it believable that all the monsters could fit inside. Thanks to some tools created before production began, the team was also able to reduce each model proportionally by ten to fifteen percent without comprising the overall fidelity.

"I loved doing this scene as the Invisible Man says goodbye to his 'invisible' girlfriend, who everyone knows doesn't exist."
— DAVID FEISS · STORY ARTIST

"If you were to pull the camera all the way out, the characters would be crashing through the floor with their feet hanging outside of the hearse."
— MICHAEL KURINSKY · PRODUCTION DESIGNER

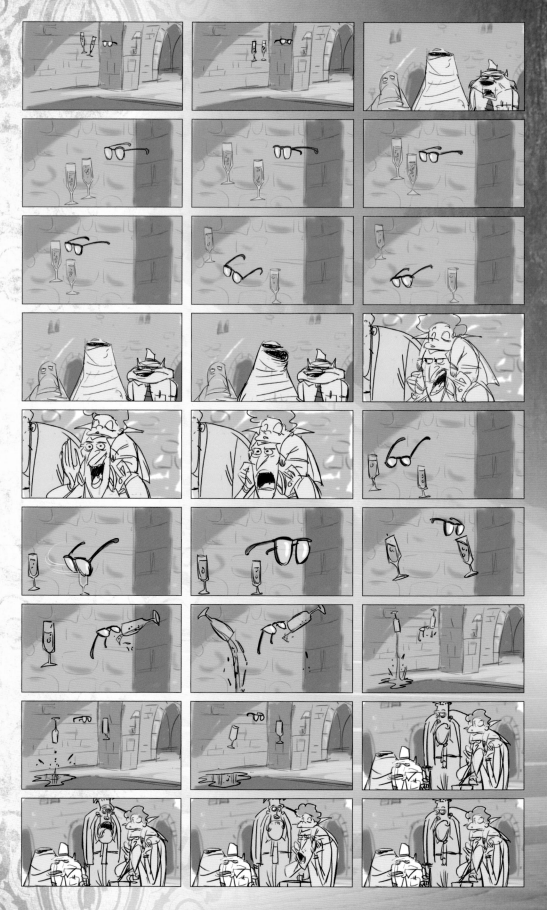

Above: *Romanian road • Michael Spooner*
Below: *Windmill • Michael Spooner*
Bottom Right: *Wind turbines • Michael Spooner*

BELOW: *Storyboard • John Norton*
RIGHT: *Lighting keys • Chin Ko*
OPPOSITE TOP RIGHT: *Dog park • Michael Spooner (design), Michael Kurinsky (paint)*
OPPOSITE BOTTOM: *Lighting keys • Michael Kurinsky & Aurélien Predal*

THE DARK FOREST OF SLOBOZIA

PRIOR TO REACHING THE CAMP, the gang makes a stop at the supposedly spooky and imposing Dark Forest of Slobozia, a place where Dracula used to get into monster mischief when he was still in his hundreds. Back then it was a moor, complete with low mists and very creepy trees.

As with the rest of the present-day world, things aren't entirely what they used to be. Instead of a foreboding, spooky space, the forest has become a dog park of sorts, where humans and their pets can take a nice stroll. It's well lit and surrounded by pretty flowers. "It's like a little oasis of friendly humanness in the middle of a Transylvanian forest," explains production designer Michael Kurinsky.

Similar to the beginning of the movie, which uses a lot of traveling shots as the characters approach the castle for the first time, the team first framed the forest to look foreboding—it is very desaturated and misty, and dark silhouettes of trees abound. Once the characters emerge into the park and it becomes apparent that things have changed, the lighting quickly becomes artificially warm, revealing a lot of brightly colored flowers all around.

The park location gives Frank, Wayne, and Murray an opportunity to show off their special scaring techniques. "Everybody gets a moment to show off what they do really well," explains Kurinsky. "Frank shows how to scare people, Wayne shows how to kill and eat a whole deer, and Murray conjures up a giant swarm of locusts."

Dracula thinks he and his friends have a foolproof plan for making the forest scary again, but it blows up in his face. As it turns out, each of them has forgotten how to be a monster—they've all been humanized.

FRANK PRACTICES HIS SCARE TECHNIQUE AS JOGGERS APPROACH.

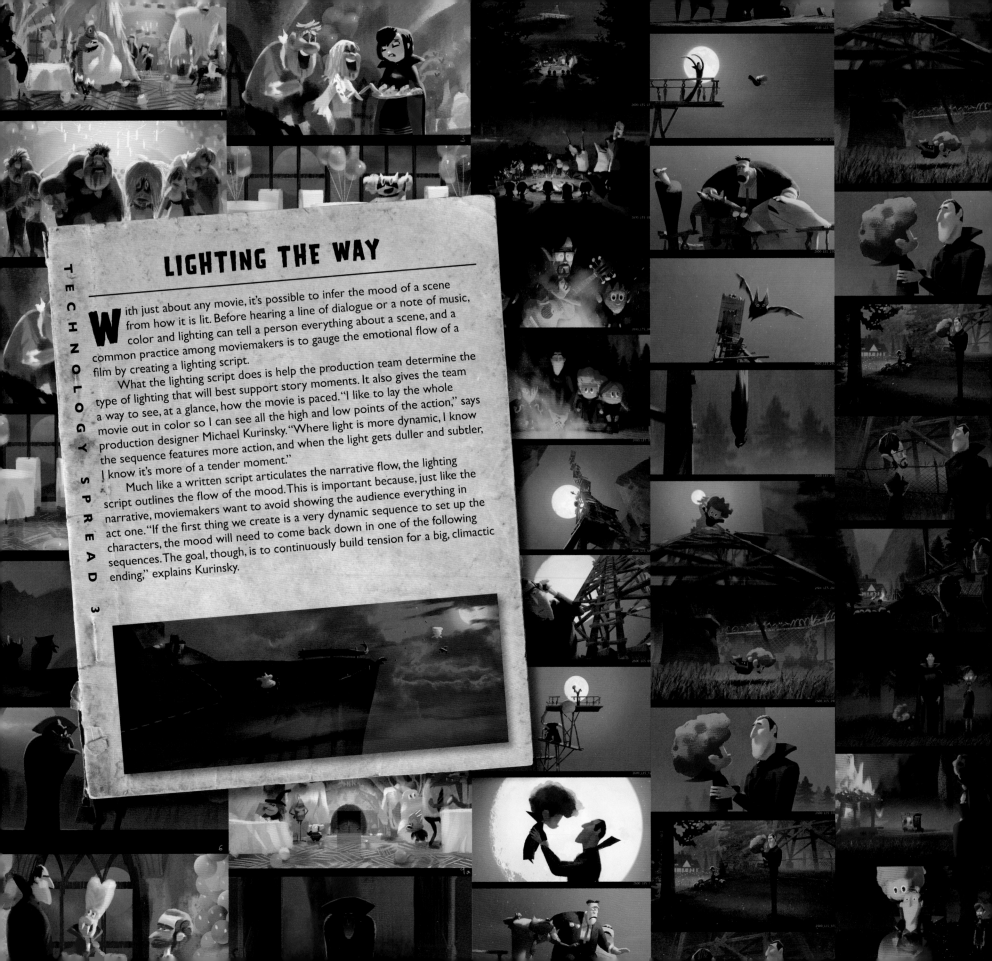

LIGHTING THE WAY

With just about any movie, it's possible to infer the mood of a scene from how it is lit. Before hearing a line of dialogue or a note of music, color and lighting can tell a person everything about a scene, and a common practice among moviemakers is to gauge the emotional flow of a film by creating a lighting script.

What the lighting script does is help the production team determine the type of lighting that will best support story moments. It also gives the team a way to see, at a glance, how the movie is paced. "I like to lay the whole movie out in color so I can see all the high and low points of the action," says production designer Michael Kurinsky. "Where light is more dynamic, I know the sequence features more action, and when the light gets duller and subtler, I know it's more of a tender moment."

Much like a written script articulates the narrative flow, the lighting script outlines the flow of the mood. This is important because, just like the narrative, moviemakers want to avoid showing the audience everything in act one. "If the first thing we create is a very dynamic sequence to set up the characters, the mood will need to come back down in one of the following sequences. The goal, though, is to continuously build tension for a big, climactic ending," explains Kurinsky.

OPPOSITE: *Lighting keys* • *Aurélien Predal*
OPPOSITE (INSET): *Lighting key* • *Michael Kurinsky*
ABOVE & BELOW: *Lighting keys* • *Michael Kurinsky,*
Aurélien Predal, Chin Ko, Miguel Gil

CAMP WINNEPACACA

IN A LAST-DITCH EFFORT to show Dennis what it means to be a monster, Dracula takes the gang to the vampire camp he attended in his youth. There, he hopes to expose Dennis to all manner of activities tailored specifically for young vampire children. "We do a complete misdirect upon their arrival, however," explains production designer Michael Kurinsky. "We show a flashback of how Dracula used to remember the camp when he attended, and it's changed quite a bit. Hundreds of years ago the entire area was more foreboding and menacing, but now it's a very pleasant place, complete with twinkly lights and children playing badminton."

Camp Winnepacaca, or Camp Vamp as it's now known, was the first new location designed for the movie when production started. Before diving headfirst into development, Kurinsky took a moment to create a backstory for the place. In his mind, the camp was a place that had existed for a long time, possibly thousands of years. So he asked himself: How is it possible that the location was never discovered? And how is it that sunlight has never been a factor?

What he and the team came up with is a camp surrounded two-thirds of the way around by stone walls that are roughly 10,000 feet high. Additionally, the camp is located in a hidden valley that is accessible only via treacherous and windy roads. The only reason the valley isn't completely surrounded by walls is the team wanted to leave a sliver of an opening so the jump tower could be silhouetted against the light of the moon.

"We designed the camp in a secluded area nestled in a deep valley, to ensure the monsters would be hidden from humans."
— AURORA JIMENEZ · VISUAL DEVELOPMENT ARTIST

GORDON '13

ABOVE & OPPOSITE BOTTOM:
Camp exteriors • Aurora Jimenez
BELOW: *Main house exterior • Michael Kurinsky*

COUNSELOR DANA AND THE VAMPIRE KIDS

For the camp counselor, Dana, the team initially found inspiration in Al Lewis, the late actor who played Grandpa in the television show *The Munsters* (1964). Yet instead of having a goofy, warm personality like Lewis's character, they wanted to make the counselor a tough, crotchety old man.

As the team began to iterate on Dana, they decided that the Al Lewis–inspired approach was too much like the old-guard vampires who used to run the camp. The present-day Dana needed to be gentler and passive to reflect the new age of monster.

After exploring skinny and waifish versions, the team ultimately decided on a rounder, softer, and gentler character design for Dana, making him into someone who essentially embodies everything that Dracula despises. As production designer Michael Kurinsky points out, "If the camp has truly changed, the people who are running it should be more sensitive and caring."

To create the vampire kids attending Winnepacaca, the team took a Frankenstein approach by using parts of a few models, and then mixing and matching them to create a legion of campers.

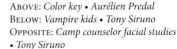

ABOVE: *Color key • Aurélien Predal*
BELOW: *Vampire kids • Tony Siruno*
OPPOSITE: *Camp counselor facial studies • Tony Siruno*

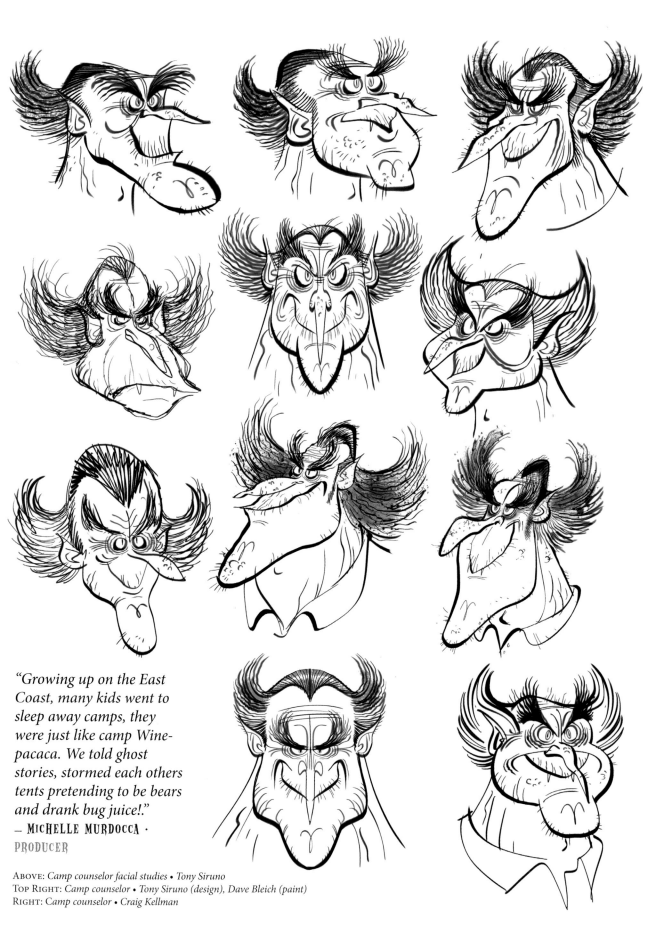

"Growing up on the East Coast, many kids went to sleep away camps, they were just like camp Wine-pacaca. We told ghost stories, stormed each others tents pretending to be bears and drank bug juice!"
— MICHELLE MURDOCCA ·
PRODUCER

ABOVE: *Camp counselor facial studies* • Tony Siruno
TOP RIGHT: *Camp counselor* • Tony Siruno (design), Dave Bleich (paint)
RIGHT: *Camp counselor* • Craig Kellman

RIGHT: *Bunkhouse exterior • Michael Kurinsky (design), Dean Gordon (paint)*
BELOW: *Bunkhouse interior • Dean Gordon*

THE UNDEAD CAMP

THE INITIAL DIRECTION for the main house was to make it look like a typical haunted house. After some consideration, though, director Genndy Tartakovsky felt that it should be part haunted house and part something you would find in a wilderness, camp-like setting. The final look incorporates a creepy face to give it a "scare" factor while the structure is made out of rustic, old wood that's twisted and gnarled.

The bunkhouses are very similar to the main house in their construction, and both are painted black. Inside are special bunk beds that are made out of logs and fashioned to look like coffins. Like the structures, they are the perfect blend of "monster meets wilderness that Genndy was looking for," says production designer Michael Kurinsky.

Top: *Camp main house • Dean Gordon*
Top Right: *Main house model • Michael Kurinsky*
Bottom left: *Camp exterior • Michael Kurinsky*
Bottom Right: *Lighting key • Michael Kurinsky*

WINNEPACACA

BELOW: *Storyboards • Graham Keith Baxter*
RIGHT: *New jump tower • Seonna Hong*
FAR RIGHT (& INSETS): *Jump tower and schematics • Aurora Jimenez*
OPPOSITE TOP: *Jump tower • Michael Spooner*
OPPOSITE BOTTOM: *Jump tower base • Aurora Jimenez*

THE JUMP TOWER

THE OLD JUMP TOWER is the only element of the camp that conforms to how Dracula remembers it. However, it hasn't been used for hundreds of years and is dilapidated, standing precariously where it always has—a reminder of the good old days.

Nearby, a new jump tower that is decidedly less imposing and dangerous has been set up. It stands only a few feet above the ground and has a protective, bouncy mattress underneath it to ensure young vampires don't get hurt.

Dracula takes Dennis to the old jump tower to try to teach him how to turn into a bat and fly. However, as with most things on their journey, the end result isn't what Dracula intended. Frank inadvertently catches fire and proceeds to bring the whole structure crashing to the ground. "It was a really big effects sequence with a lot of destruction," explains visual effects supervisor Karl Herbst. "The trick for us was to find a balance between photorealism and the animation style defined by our motion language. When it comes to effects, Genndy likes to give a Tex Avery–style flair to certain things. When the simulation team shows me dust hits, for example, I add a little 'zing' to it."

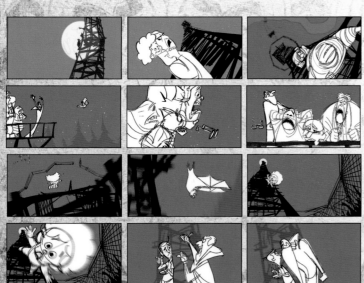

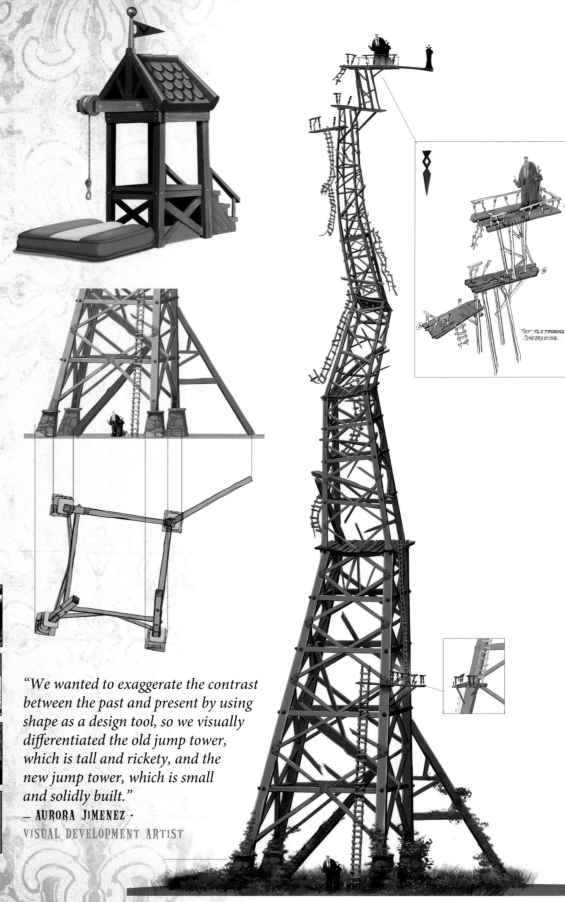

"We wanted to exaggerate the contrast between the past and present by using shape as a design tool, so we visually differentiated the old jump tower, which is tall and rickety, and the new jump tower, which is small and solidly built."

— AURORA JIMENEZ ·
VISUAL DEVELOPMENT ARTIST

TOP PLATFORMS
3/4 DRAWING

ACT
3

THE ART OF ANIMATION

As a visionary director and twenty-year veteran of the art, director Genndy Tartakovsky is an inspiration to the entire animation team. During development on *Hotel Transylvania 2*, he was constantly teaching and encouraging the animators to take characters in bold directions. To say the team enjoys working alongside Tartakovsky is certainly an understatement.

"I often have an idea in my head of what I want. So when the animation team puts something in front of me, I will draw over the image to show them how to push what's there a little bit more. Some stuff's real simple, such as working on an expression. In other instances, there may be a character onscreen who's getting pushed out of a doorway and I want the body language to be accentuated or exaggerated a bit more," explains Tartakovsky.

For example, when a character reaches for a phone in perhaps another animated film, the movement may look very human-like. But in the *Hotel Transylvania* world, everything is more cartoony and caricatured. "In our world, if someone picks up a phone, I want the animators to add a little flourish to the movement. It's a very old-school Tex Avery, Warner Bros. approach to animation," continues Tartakovsky.

In a sense, the draw-overs are how Tartakovsky directs. "The draw-overs are Genndy's way of giving us notes," explains animation supervisor Alan Hawkins "We show him some poses and he makes improvements with quick pen strokes. We can then take those images and put them right into our workflow as reference, trace what he's done, and then show him what we came up with."

However, even with the ability to add Tartakovsky's work into a scene as a reference point, it's still hard to incorporate. "The computer-generated version underneath the draw-over does what the rig wants to do," says Hawkins. "To get the model to do what Genndy wants it to, the animation team often has to tweak and re-sculpt the asset." While this can be a difficult undertaking, the end results are characters imbued with unique personalities and an animation style that's distinct to the *Hotel Transylvania* movies.

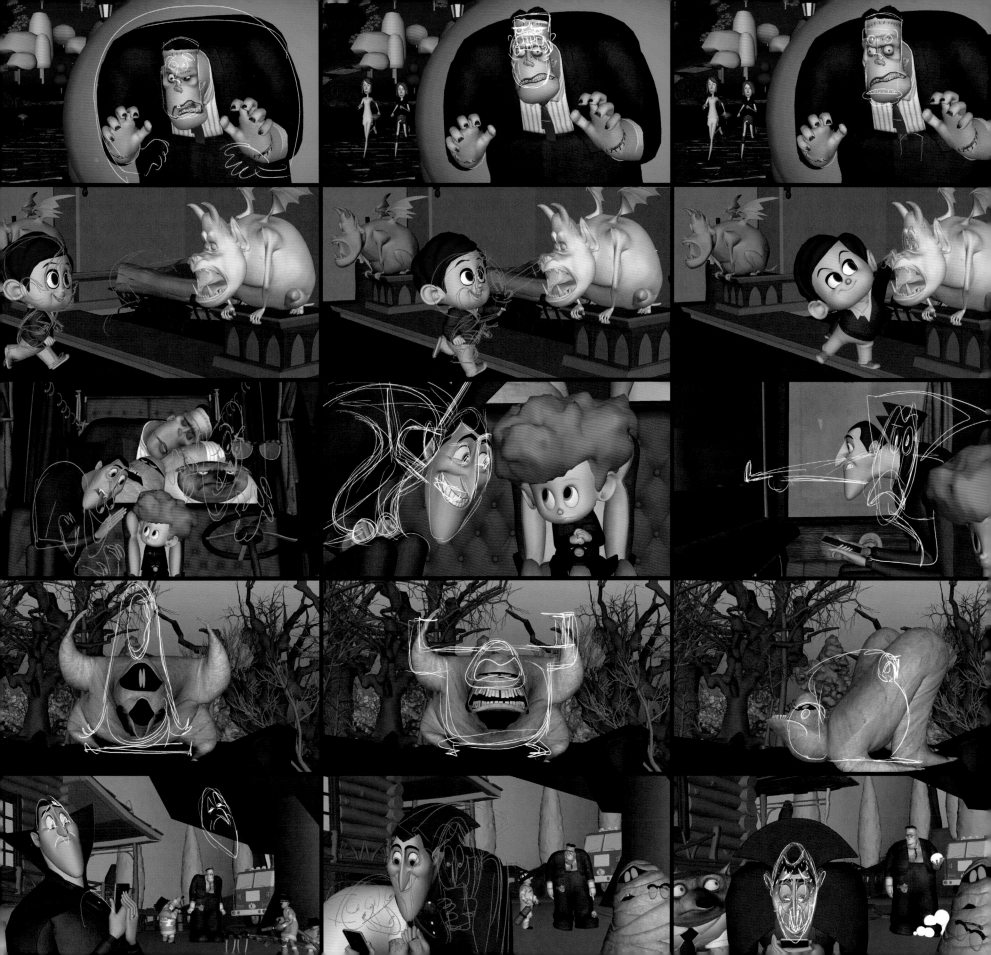

THE AIRPORT

RIGHT: *Airport interior • Jim Alles*
FAR RIGHT: *Airport exterior • Jim Alles*

TO DESIGN THE AIRPORT, the team took the same approach they did with the rest of the human world, which was to create a very straightforward, horizontal environment. Since Johnny is from Santa Cruz, the design for the structure is based off of the San Jose airport in Northern California—the closest international airport to Santa Cruz. The team took the location as a starting point, embellishing and exaggerating it to create a look that is distinct but also reminiscent of the actual airport.

The lighting for the airport is on par with the lighting used throughout the human world as well. In a conscious effort to create a feeling of familiarity, "we intentionally used fluorescent lights so it doesn't feel warm and inviting," explains production designer Michael Kurinsky.

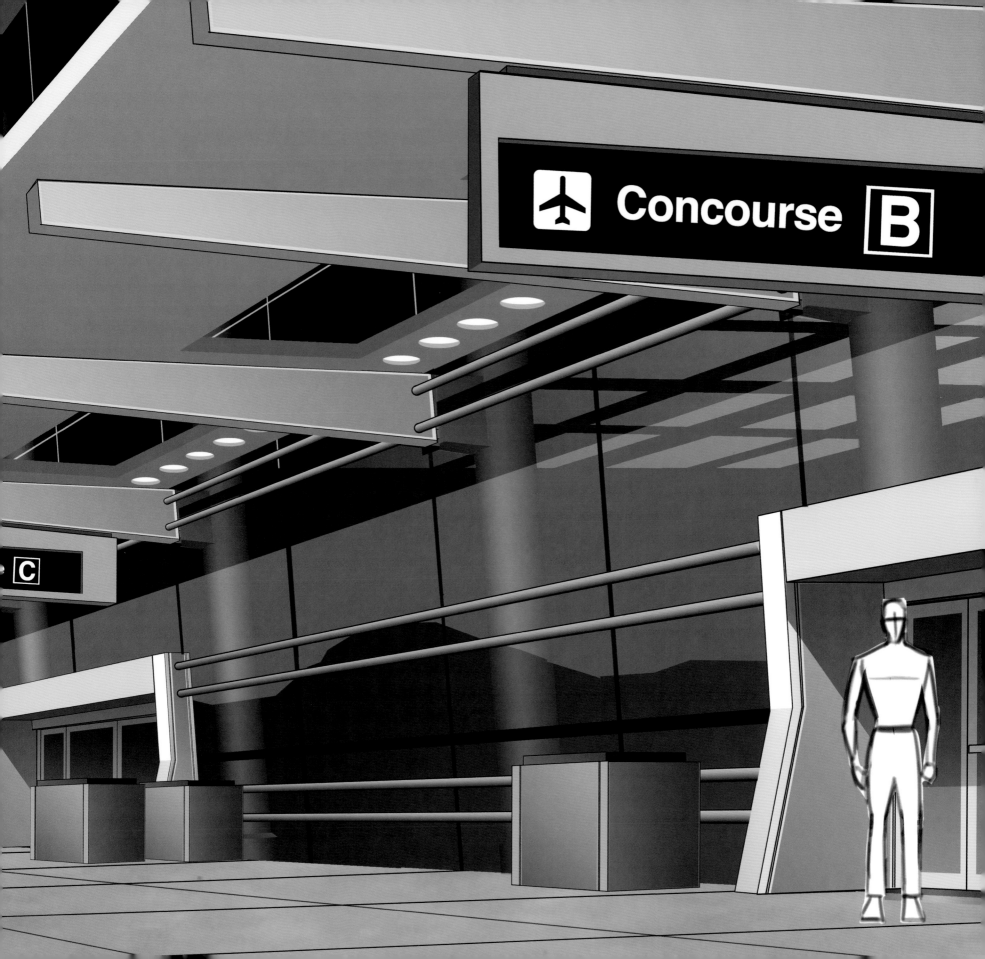

ABOVE: *Mavis and Johnny on the 'flight' home* • Steve Lumley
BELOW: *Airport exterior* • Jim Alles (design), Miguel Gil (paint)

VLAD'S LAIR

WHEN IT CAME TO DESIGNING where Vlad lives, the production team initially thought he should inhabit an old-school castle—in other words, a classic foreboding location right out of a vampire movie from the twentieth century. "When we first got the script, we did some classic designs," recalls production designer Michael Kurinsky.

At the same time, the team was also fleshing out who Vlad was as a character. During the explorations, director Genndy Tartakovsky thought he should be more of a hermit, rather than an opposing overlord of the dark realm. This led to discussions about him living in a cave underground without a dining room, fancy parlor, or amenities of any kind. In fact, the only piece of furniture Vlad has is a large throne made from the stone found inside the cave.

As the team continued exploring variations of what the cave could look like, they came to the conclusion that it didn't need to be a very big place. "We felt the cave should be very stifling and have a very low ceiling. It's not an open space, by any means," says Kurinsky.

Despite the small footprint, it took a while to create Vlad's cavernous domain. "It's supposed to feel like slate, so we needed to create flaky-looking rock, which is not easy to model and light," explains visual effects supervisor Karl Herbst. "We spent a lot of time sculpting to get it just right."

Once the design was established, it was time to think about color. As Kurinsky explains, color scripting was influential when it came to introducing Vlad's character. "We start on the outside at night with very warm colors, and as we go down into the bowels of the cave, the color gets colder and colder. By the time we arrive at the bottom, the scene has changed to a very cold, blue color," he says.

The color choices help establish a mood that is very cold, supporting the idea that Vlad is a curmudgeonly old guy. "Vlad lives in a slate cave; it's not pretty in the slightest. It says a lot about the person who lives there—he wants to be left alone."

116

THIS PAGE: *Vlad's lair • Sylvain Marc*

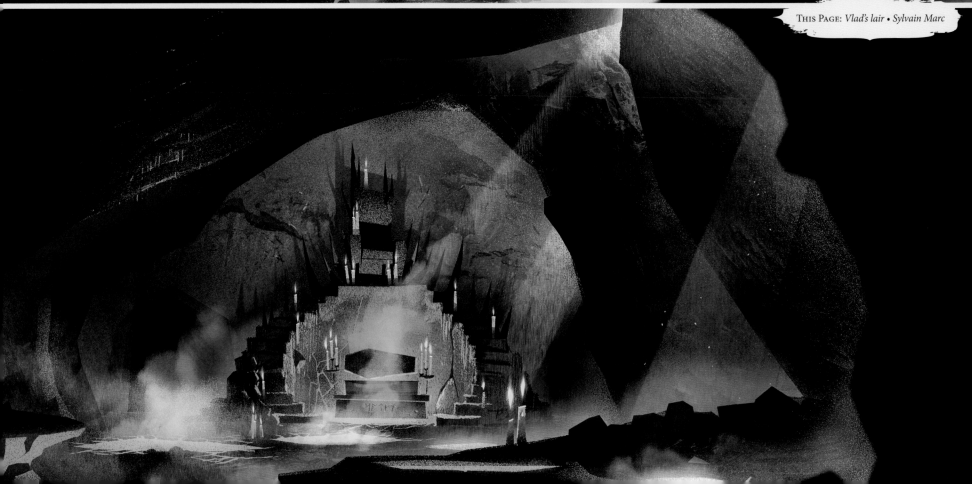

"Vlad's lair was strongly influenced by the work of Ken Adam, who designed the iconic lairs for the James Bond villains of the 1960s and 1970s."
— JAMES WILLIAMS · LAYOUT ARTIST

TOP ROW: *Vlad's lair* • Sylvain Marc
MIDDLE ROW: *Vlads' lair* • Steve Lumley
LEFT: *Vlads' crypt* • Steve Lumley
RIGHT: *Vlads' throne* • Sylvain Marc
(design), Todd Gibbs (paint)

"The cave is very simple, and the perfect retreat for a secluded old, grumpy vampire."
— SYLVAIN MARC · VISUAL DEVELOPMENT ARTIST

WHO'S YOUR VLADDY?

WHEN DESIGNING VLAD, director Genndy Tartakovsky worked closely with character designer Craig Kellman to get the character's features and proportions just right. "I wanted his shape to be reminiscent of Dracula, since Vlad is his dad, so his head is shaped much like a coffin," explains Tartakovsky. "He needed to be super crotchety and super old, somewhere along the lines of 5,000 years old or thereabouts, so visually the character needed to reflect that."

As is evident from the artwork, Vlad is definitely creepier, more decrepit, and a little bonier than his son. There is also a little bit more detail in Vlad's skin than there is in Dracula's, which is very smooth. The product of an intense development process, Vlad's final design can handle the full range of expressions and emotions needed from the character—whether creepy or kooky.

As animation supervisor Alan Hawkins recalls, "We didn't have the character to work with during our usual ramp-up period, which is normally when we perform character-development tests. Since we were well into production, we just did some broad posing with him, he wasn't in motion—it was all about shapes. But that turned out to be fine because that's the way Genndy thinks. It's all about lines and shapes first, and then about mechanics."

Once Hawkins and his team were up and running with an actual model, Tartakovsky had already established rules for Vlad's movements that were very different from the snappy, quick movements typical of most characters in the *Hotel Transylvania* movies. "Everything about Vlad is very articulated and slow, until there is action onscreen that warrants faster movement," Tartakovsky explains. "If I see animation that's too fast, we look to slow it down. Vlad needs to feel different, more controlled." This ponderous pace puts Vlad in sharp contrast with Dracula, who's very manic and always zipping around.

TOP RIGHT: *Storyboards* • *Dave Krentz*
BOTTOM RIGHT: *Storyboards* • *Denise Koyama*
OPPOSITE LEFT: *Vlad sketches* • *Andre Medina*
OPPOSITE FAR RIGHT: *Vlad* • *Craig Kellman (design), Seonna Hong (paint)*

"As we began to develop Vlad's character, he became a hermit who lives in an underground lair—his posture is very indicative of that."
— ANDRE MEDINA · VISUAL DEVELOPMENT ARTIST

"Vlad is a guy with a lot of wrinkles, a lot of wear-and-tear on his body. We went as far as to put cobwebs on his cape; he's dirty, old, and crusty."
— MICHAEL KURINSKY · PRODUCTION DESIGNER

THIS SPREAD: *Vlad character sketches • Andre Medina & Craig Kellman*

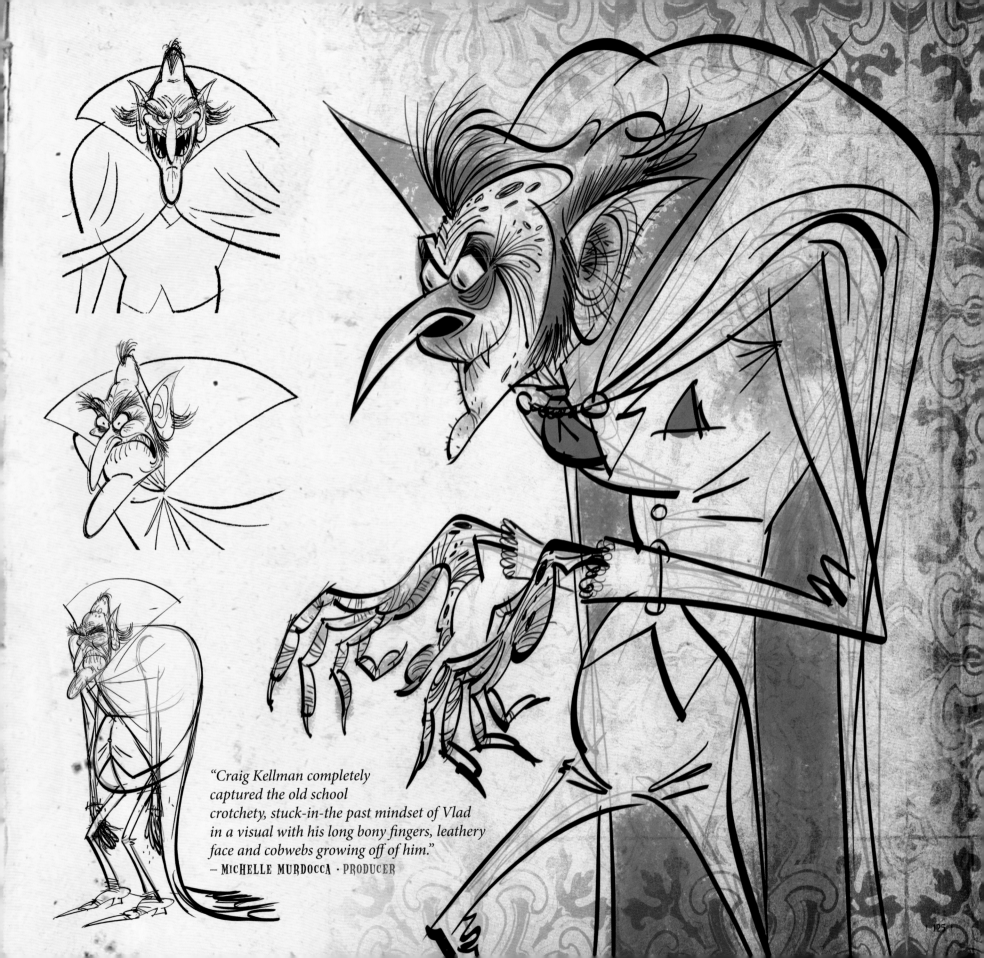

"Craig Kellman completely captured the old school crotchety, stuck-in-the past mindset of Vlad in a visual with his long bony fingers, leathery face and cobwebs growing off of him."
— MICHELLE MURDOCCA · PRODUCER

"In Vlad's lair there are more than 150 cronies in some shots."
— JAMES WILLIAMS · LAYOUT ARTIST

BAD BATS

ORIGINALLY, Vlad was supposed to be the most terrifying character in *Hotel Transylvania 2*, but that honorific eventually went to his lieutenant, Bela. "He is sort of second-in-command, next to Vlad," explains production designer Michael Kurinsky. "However, even though Bela goes along with Vlad and listens to everything he says, we set up the relationship so you always feel like he's right on the edge of wanting to take the throne. There's a tension between the two of them that is very palpable."

In addition to Bela, there are a host of other Vlad cronies that lurk in the shadows. When these bad bats first appear in his cave, they are nothing more than sets of red eyes glowing in the darkness. Unlike Bela, the cronies have no interest in taking control; they are content to be monstrous bullies, braying and cackling at anything the two alpha vampires say.

"When creating these characters, we wanted them to be scary and intimidating, but not so much so that we terrify the kids in the audience," explains director Genndy Tartakovsky. "To take the edge off Bela's appearance, we make him act and walk a little bit sillier than you would otherwise expect. If we hadn't made this choice, people would really be scared."

One unique aspect of Bela and the cronies is the way their models were constructed. Rather than build them as they would a normal animated character, Genndy decided he wanted to add a touch more visual menace to their appearance by making them more realistic. "One of the new techniques we tried was to create a muscle system for these characters, which is something you would see in a live-action movie," says Tartakovsky. "There's actually a muscular structure rig underneath their skin, so when they move their arms and stomachs you can see their arm and abdominal muscles flex," adds Kurinsky.

TOP LEFT, BOTTOM LEFT, ABOVE & LEFT: *Crony sketches* • *Stephen DeStefano*
MIDDLE: *Bela color study* • *Chin Ko*

BELOW: *Crony • Joey Chou*
TOP RIGHT: *Crony sketches • Stephen DeStefano*
BOTTOM RIGHT: *Crony • Stephen DeStefano*
OPPOSITE: *Bela • Stephen DeStefano (design),*
Michael Kurinsky (paint)

"When caricatured characters do scary things, it's not as scary."
— GENNDY TARTAKOVSKY •
DIRECTOR

LATE FANGER

When Dracula became concerned that Dennis was a "late fanger," he decided the best, most subtle way to coax his grandson's fangs to drop would be to show Dennis acts of monsterism with the help of Frank, Wayne, and Murray. This, of course, yielded less-than-desired results. As it turns out, Dracula was also a "late fanger." Unfortunately for Dracula, Vlad's way of coaxing his fangs out was a little more extreme. To put it lightly, take something that Dracula loves and turn it into something terrifying. The object of young Dracula's affection, as it turns out, was a baby raccoon.

"We made the raccoon look super cute, much like Hello Kitty," explains director Genndy Tartakovsky. "Right away we put the kids in the audience at ease. Since Dracula was born thousands of years ago, the imagery is done in black and white, giving the scene an 'old-world' feeling," he continues. "All of a sudden (the raccoon's) head turns around and it becomes demonized after a full revolution, complete with red eyes, giant fangs, and claws," adds production designer Michael Kurinsky. The raccoon that was once cute is horrifying, which induces Dracula into a state where his fangs come out. Even though the scare "is intense, there's still an element of silliness to it," concludes Tartakovsky.

"I based the possessed raccoon design on a rabid opossum—the kind I would find early in the morning while riding my bike to school."
— ANDRE MEDINA ·
VISUAL DEVELOPMENT
ARTIST

OPPOSITE TOP & BOTTOM: *Young Dracula's bedroom • Aurora Jimenez*
ABOVE: *Demonic raccoon • Andre Medina (design), Kristy Kay (paint)*
ABOVE RIGHT: *Raccoon • Andre Medina*
RIGHT: *Storyboards • Paul Watling*
FAR RIGHT: *Demonic raccoon • Andre Medina*

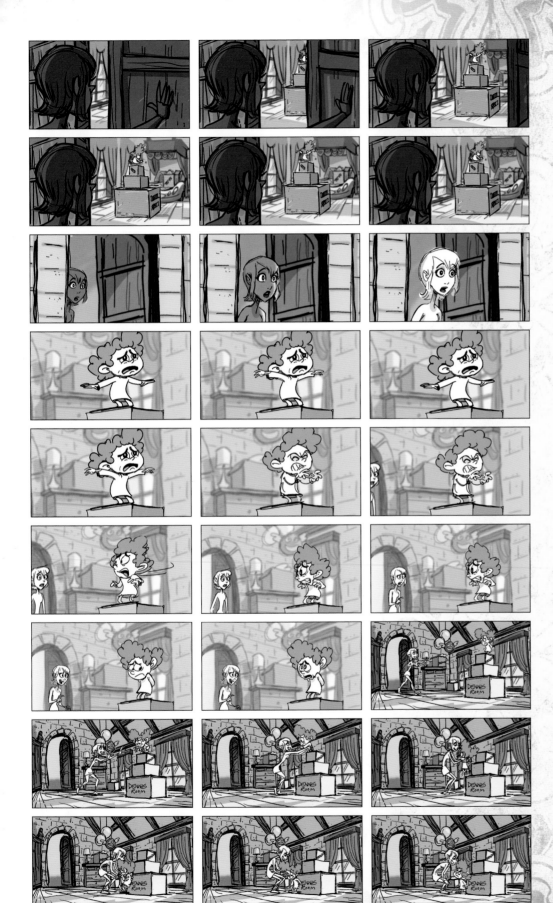

PACKING UP

Since it seems that Dennis is destined to be human like Johnny, Mavis decides it would be better if they all moved to California so that Dennis can be around "normal" people like him. "We really wanted to create a somber scene," recalls production designer Michael Kurinsky. "And I had an idea that the scene should take place during the daytime, which is something you don't see at all in the *Hotel Transylvania* movies. Fortunately, director Genndy Tartakovsky was on board with the concept."

To get around the fact that Mavis can't walk around during the daytime, Kurinsky proposed that the weather outside be overcast and raining. That way, any light coming into the castle would be diminished by the clouds. Additionally, they decided that there shouldn't be any lights on inside Johnny and Mavis's suite. Doing this allowed any light coming in from outside to cast a shadow of rain on the wall, symbolizing tears dripping down the windows and adding to the emotion of the scene.

"This is as somber and desaturated as we've ever seen it in the monster world."
— Michael Kurinsky · Production Designer

"Good direction and storytelling is knowing when to take an intimate moment and stage it so the audience is emotionally engaged with the characters on screen."
— Darrell Rooney · Story Artist

Left: *Storyboards* • *Darrell Rooney*
Opposite Top & Bottom: *Color keys* • *Michael Kurinsky*

DINNER IS SERVED

Phantom of the Opera

THE DINING ROOM for Dennis's party is one of the few rooms in the hotel that production designer Michael Kurinsky got to build from the ground up. "This is a new space in the hotel; we weren't just taking a place in the castle and redressing it—we were actually tasked with designing a new room, which was very exciting," he says.

When Kurinsky first read the script, he instantly knew that the birthday party was going to be an extremely intense scene. To start, the team made the room oval-shaped and added stylized buttresses, creating a claustrophobic feeling. "By their very nature, they make it feel like something is looming over the people in the room. And to push that idea a bit further, we added high-backed chairs so that there would be this feeling that something was always looking down and encroaching." To top it all off, a Phantom of the Opera in the room plays an organ loudly and sings at the top of his lungs.

As for lighting, the choice was rather easy. Again, while reading the script, Kurinsky began jotting down color and lighting notes. "My first impression was red," he recalls. "Let's color it as red as we can."

To that end, there's a big, red tablecloth and the backs of the chairs are red. "For the big fire in the fireplace, I had the team push the color to be more orange than an actual flame would be," says Kurinsky. "So there's a red cast to the whole room."

JOHNNY'S EXTENDED FAMILY ARRIVES FOR DINNER.

"It's a perfect marriage: from the claustrophobic way the room is constructed to the color of the lighting. All of it works to create the tension the team was going for."
— MICHAEL KURINSKY · PRODUCTION DESIGNER

OPPOSITE BOTTOM LEFT: *Storyboard* • *John Norton*
OPPOSITE TOP: *Phantom of the Opera* • *Craig Kellman*
OPPOSITE BOTTOM RIGHT: *Lighting keys* • *Miguel Gil*
ABOVE: *Dining room* • *Aurora Jimenez (design), Miguel Gil (paint)*
BELOW: *Dining room fireplace* • *Aurora Jimenez*

KAKIE MONSTER!

"We created an inviting scenario where Vlad looks more like an actor in a play, rather than someone about to turn Kakie into a demonic apparition."
— AURORA JIMENEZ · VISUAL DEVELOPMENT ARTIST

SINCE DRACULA WAS UNABLE to induce Dennis's fangs to drop, he decides to resort to extreme measures and allow Vlad to perform a ritual reminiscent of what happened to his beloved raccoon on one of Dennis's favorite things: Kakie the Cake Monster. Inevitably, what starts out as a seemingly "harmless" spectacle soon takes a turn for the worse.

The event happens in the ballroom of the castle, the location of the table-flying sequence involving Dracula and Johnny in the first movie. However, the scene in *Hotel Transylvania 2* is decidedly darker in tone. To create the perfect mood, lighting was used to full effect. "There are a lot of big, emotional changes that occur during this scene," explains production designer Michael Kurinsky. "When it starts, there are a lot of hats and balloons, and the lighting is used to create a festive atmosphere."

However, the mood changes as Kakie, who is just some poor guy in a costume, and Vlad appear. At that point, the houselights drop and Kakie and Vlad are lit with a simple stage light. The scene quickly shifts from inviting to sinister as Vlad performs the same ritual on Kakie that he did on Dracula's pet raccoon, mutating the costume into a scary, hideous form. Again, red is used to create a feeling of tension. Because the purpose of the event is to scare the fangs out of Dennis, the lighting builds in intensity until, all of a sudden, the room is cast into darkness, except for the moonlight streaming through the windows.

TROY/PARKER/CONNER — "CAKEY? WHAT A WUSS-BAG!"

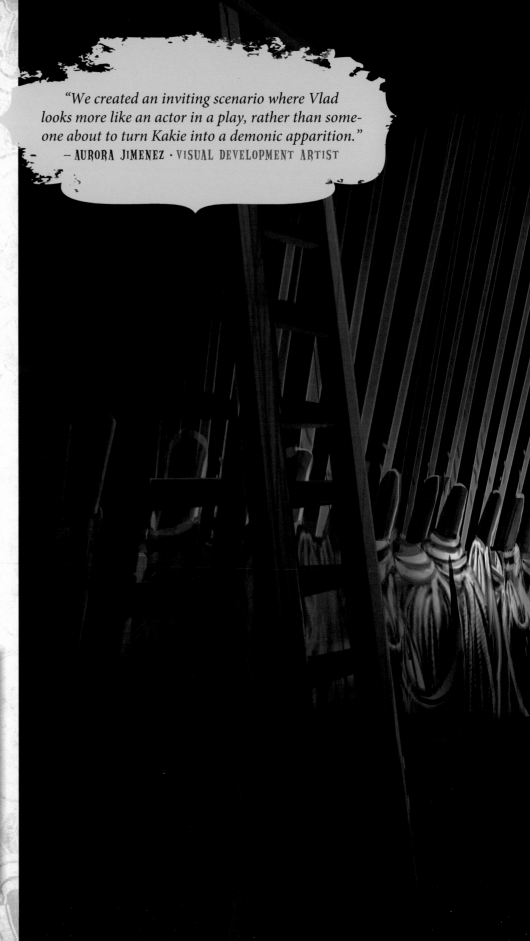

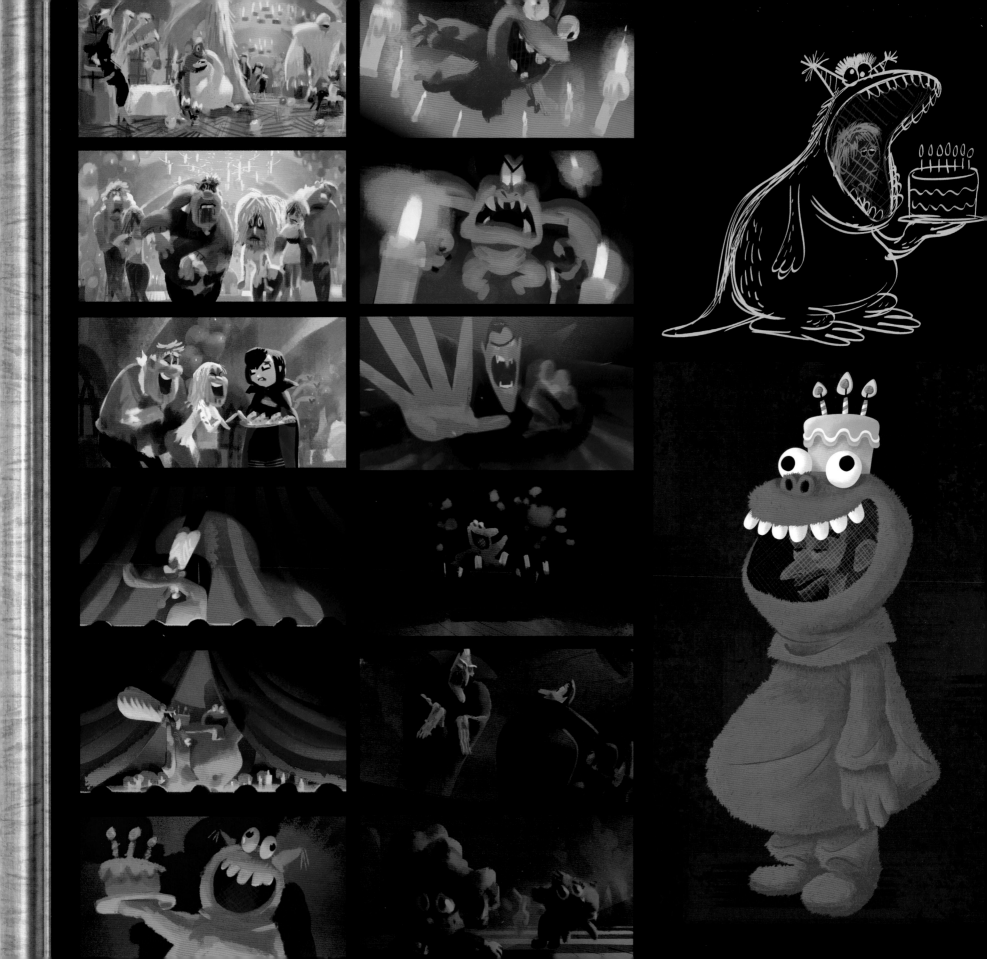

FAR LEFT: *Color keys • Aurélien Predal*
LEFT: *Kakie costume • Craig Kellman*
ABOVE: *Kakie costume • Stephen DeStefano*
RIGHT: *Demonic Kakie • Craig Kellman*

BELOW: *Dog fort interior • Steve Lumley (design), Lizzie Nichols (paint)*
RIGHT: *Dog fort model • Steve Lumley*
OPPOSITE: *Dog fort exterior • Steve Lumley*

TO THE DOG FORT!

A S THE PARTY GOES COMPLETELY HAYWIRE, Dennis flees the
ballroom to get away from the chaos. Along the way, he runs
into Winnie, who suggests they go to the dog fort to hide.

The only direction production designer Michael Kurinsky gave
to art director Steve Lumley was that "the fort shouldn't look like it was built out of meticulously
cut, lumbered wood." Instead, it needed to look like it was assembled by discarded material taken
from inside the hotel. "The backstory is that Winnie built the fort," recalls Lumley, "so it's a bit
on the rustic side. It's created with mismatched boards and materials—really anything she could
grab and take to the location."

To start, Lumley took a similar approach and began by looking through a library of assets
that already existed, including some that were created for the first movie. The final fort design
is a mix of previously created assets and new ones that match the aesthetic Lumley developed
through his repurposing. "Steve really made sure not to make anything perfectly hewn—all the
materials really look like they had been thrown away," concludes Kurinsky.

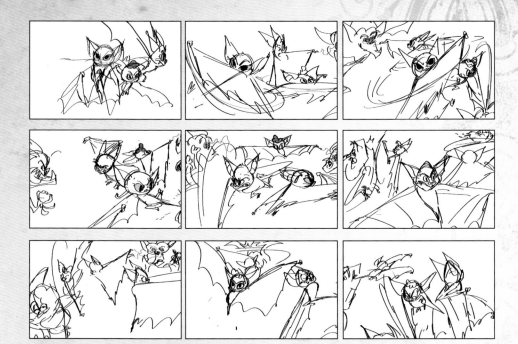

A VAMPIRE RISES!

JUST WHEN DENNIS AND WINNIE settle down in the fort, an unexpected and dangerous guest startles them. Bela has followed the two into the forest, intent on doing harm to young Dennis. In Bela's mind, Dennis is somewhat of an insult to monsterkind since the monster bloodline should be pure and free of the imperfections introduced by monster-human union. As Winnie moves into position to shield Dennis from Vlad's dangerous crony, Bela lashes out and strikes her, causing Winnie to cry out.

"Although Kakie was something that Dennis obviously loved and cared for, the thing he loves and cares for most outside of his immediate family is Winnie," says production designer Michael Kurinsky. "When Bela harms her, it is a turning point. His fangs immediately come out."

To set the mood for the fight between Dennis and Bela, color once again played an important role. In addition to having Dennis's eyes turn red like Dracula's and Mavis's when they become angry or agitated, Kurinsky recommended using a blood-red sunrise to light the battle. To create even more contrast, harsh moonlight was used to create very bright and very dark elements. "Looking at the sequence, some characters have a harsh, bright rim of moonlight across a third of their body and the rest of their body is cast in darkness. Add in a red, warm background environment, and you have a very confrontational, intense scene, which is perfect for this sequence."

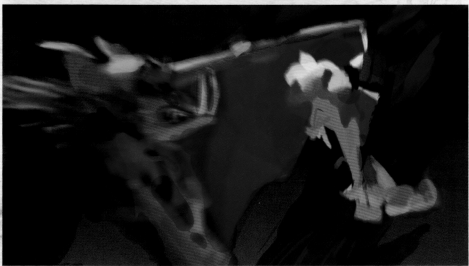

"Fighting for and protecting someone you love is more admirable than trying to scare a child."
— MICHAEL KURINSKY · PRODUCTION DESIGNER

OPPOSITE: *Dennis vampire transformation sketches* · *Craig Kellman*
TOP: *Storyboards* · *Genndy Tartakovsky*
MIDDLE & BOTTOM: *Color keys* · *Aurélien Predal*

143

"For the final battle, I incorporated red clouds in the night sky to add color diversity and intensity."
— AURÉLIEN PREDAL · VISUAL DEVELOPMENT ARTIST

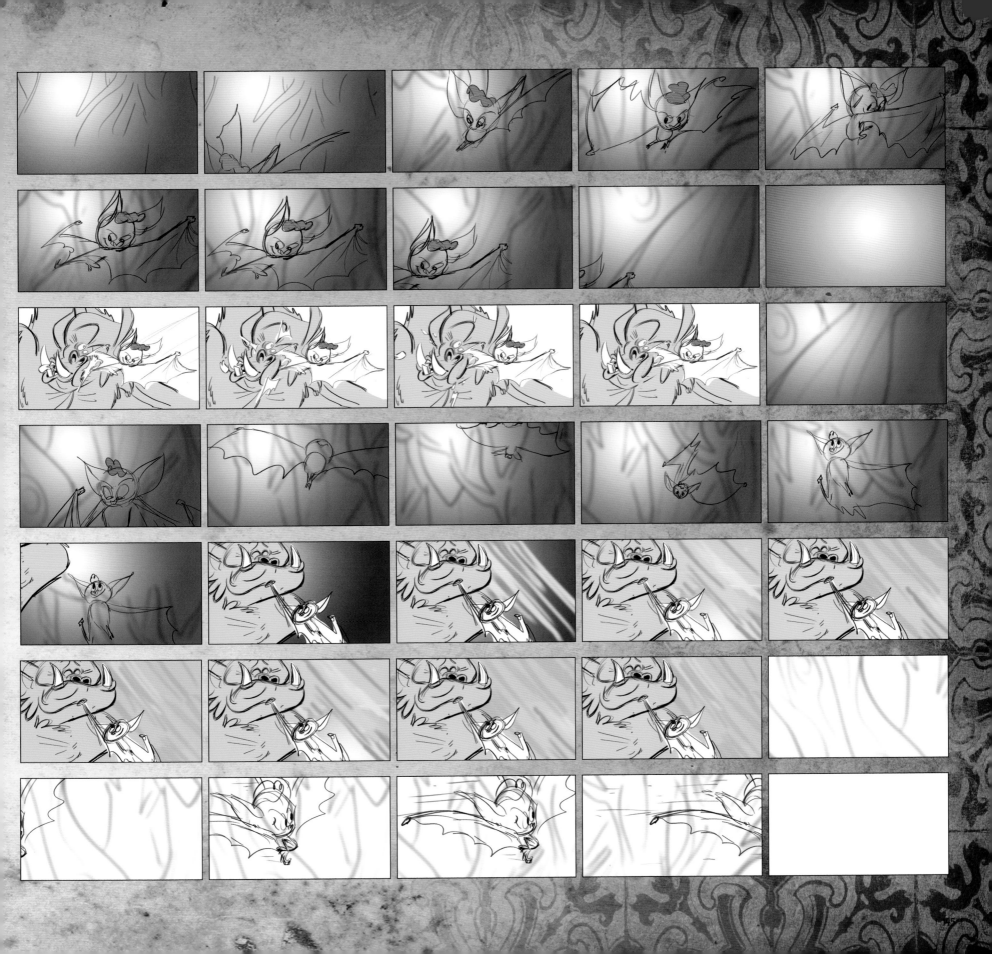

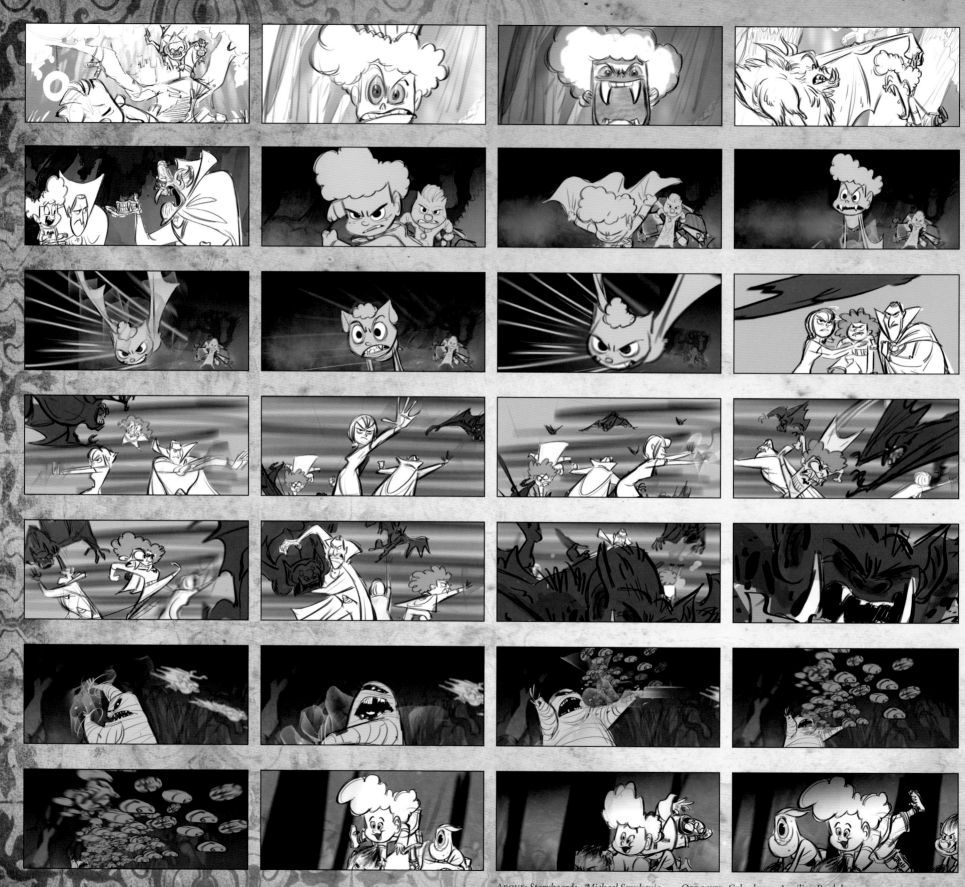

146

ABOVE: *Storyboards* • Michael Smukavic   OPPOSITE: *Color keys* • Aurélien Predal

Below: *The Lowenthals* • *Craig Kellman (design), Michael Kurinsky (paint)*
Right: *Chinese zombie* • *Stephen DeStefano (design), Chin Ko (paint)*
Opposite Top: *Talk show set* • *Michael Kurinsky*
Opposite Bottom: *Storyboards* • *Jennifer Kluska*

GONE, BUT NOT FORGOTTEN

IN MOST EVERY MOVIE, there are characters, environments, scenes, and entire plotlines that fall by the wayside, whether due to a script change, a design change, or some other creative force. Even in a world that is as fantastic and dynamic as the one in *Hotel Transylvania 2*, we find a treasure trove of unused material.

Since it would be an extreme disservice to the creative team not to share some of this unused and never-seen material, the team has dug up the following images to show what could have been. So please, sit back and relax as you turn the pages and view a special collection of artwork that represent a host of deleted or unfinished scenes that met with an untimely demise . . .

"Originally, we had the idea of showing Frank as a monster celebrity promoting his autobiography, Pieces of Me, *on a daytime talk show, while confronting Dr. Frankenstein about his traumatic 'childhood.'"*
— JENNIFER KLUSKA · STORY ARTIST

THE QUEENIE SHOW

"MY DAD BUILT ME THEN TRIED TO KILL ME!"

FRANK (OS): "You couldn't even take the time to name me!"

"MY DAD BUILT ME THEN TRIED TO KILL ME!"

"Why is MY first name, YOUR last name?!"

"MY DAD BUILT ME THEN TRIED TO KILL ME!"

"Why is MY first name, YOUR last name?!"

"MY DAD BUILT ME THEN TRIED TO KILL ME!"

"I dunno. I was busy. I was under a lot of pressure…."

"MY DAD BUILT ME THEN TRIED TO KILL ME!"

"…Ask Igor."

"MY DAD BUILT ME THEN TRIED TO KILL ME!"

"Huh…?"

"MY DAD BUILT ME THEN TRIED TO KILL ME!"

"Me…?"

"MY DAD BUILT ME THEN TRIED TO KILL ME!"

-shrug-

"MY DAD BUILT ME THEN TRIED TO KILL ME!"

"BOOOOOooooooooo…..!!!"

"MY DAD BUILT ME THEN TRIED TO KILL ME!"

(OS) "BOOOOOooooooooo…..!!!"

"MY DAD BUILT ME THEN TRIED TO KILL ME!"

"GRRrrrrrrrrr….."

"MY DAD BUILT ME THEN TRIED TO KILL ME!"

"GAAAHHHhhhhhhhhh…!!!!!!"

"MY DAD BUILT ME THEN TRIED TO KILL ME!"

"GAAAHHHhhhhhhhhh…!!!!!!"

"MY DAD BUILT ME THEN TRIED TO KILL ME!"

"GAAAHHHhhhhhhhhh…!!!!!!"

"MY DAD BUILT ME THEN TRIED TO KILL ME!"

"GAAAHHHhhhhhhhhh…!!!!!!"

"MY DAD BUILT ME THEN TRIED TO KILL ME!"

"AAAAAAaackkkk!!!"

"MY DAD BUILT ME THEN TRIED TO KILL ME!"

--Crowd shouts!--

"MY DAD BUILT ME THEN TRIED TO KILL ME!"

--Crowd shouts!--

"MY DAD BUILT ME THEN TRIED TO KILL ME!"

"MY DAD BUILT ME THEN TRIED TO KILL ME!"

"…ugh…"

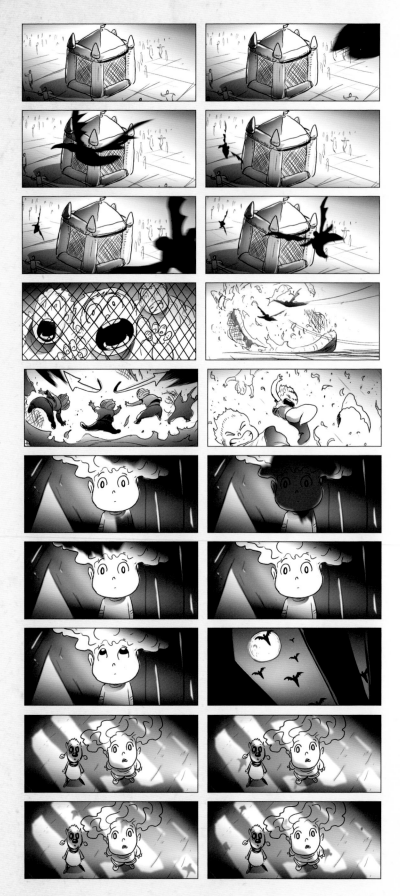

"*I wanted to make this drink look appetizing but also completely within the world of the monsters. A monster on vacation would want eyeballs and gooey stuff in his drink, but also a festive umbrella.*"
— LIZZIE NICHOLS · VISUAL DEVELOPMENT ARTIST

ABOVE: *Mall-Mart* • Aurora Jimenez
LEFT: *Chunky cocktail* • Lizzie Nichols
RIGHT: *Monster party ballroom* • Aurélien Predal

ABOVE: *Spammy* • *Tony Siruno*
BELOW: *Mr. Pickles* • *Andre Medina*
(design), Kristy Kay (paint)
RIGHT: *Quinston* • *Craig Kellman*

"Mr. Pickles was originally supposed to be a ghost cat of a ghost couple, the Lowenthals. I secretly wish my cat looked like this."
—KRISTY KAY · VISUAL DEVELOPMENT ARTIST

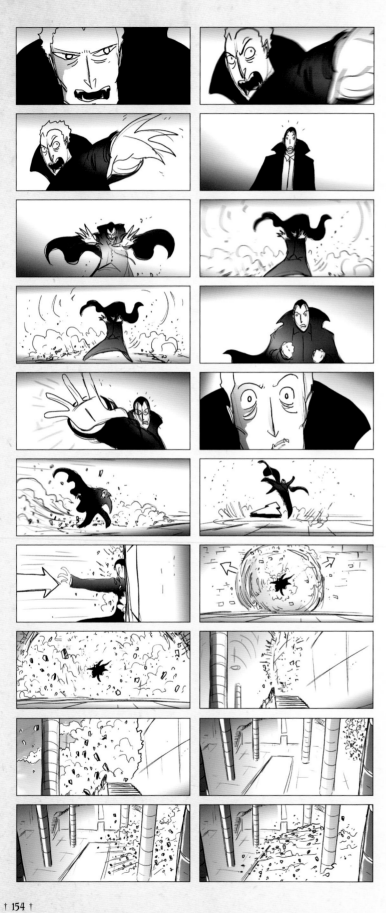

LEFT: *Storyboards* • Bryan Andrews
RIGHT: *Lobby destruction* • Sylvain Marc

ACKNOWLEDGMENTS

I WANT TO SEND MY SINCERE thanks and gratitude to all the talented moviemakers at Sony Pictures Animation for making my stay at *Hotel Transylvania* very warm and welcome. I also want to thank director Genndy Tartakovsky, producer Michelle Murdocca, production designer Michael Kurinsky, visual effects supervisor Karl Herbst, animation supervisor Alan Hawkins, and the rest of the production team for taking valuable time out of their days to speak with me and help bring this book to life. Very special thanks to Melissa Sturm for her time and help throughout the entire process.

I also want to sincerely thank Chris Gruener and Iain Morris and Cameron + Company for giving me this incredible opportunity. I am forever grateful. Finally, I would like to thank Jake Gerli. Your editorial prowess is second to none!

Lastly, I want to thank my beautiful wife, Jennifer. You truly are my zing!

Brett Rector

BRETT RECTOR has lived his life absorbing pop culture in all its wondrous forms and has had the privilege to make his livelihood writing about and creating video games. He has previously authored numerous game-related articles for *GamePro* magazine, strategy guides for Prima Games, instruction manuals for LucasArts Entertainment, and co-authored *The Art and Making of Star Wars: The Force Unleashed*. Brett has also served as the editor-in-chief of *Star Wars Insider* magazine, and has been a producer at LucasArts, where he worked on *The Force Unleashed*, *The Force Unleashed 2*, and *Lego Star Wars III: The Clone Wars*. Brett lives in San Francisco, California.

ABOVE: *Todd • Todd Gibbs*
RIGHT: *Final frame*
OVERLEAF: *Workout room • Kristy Kay*

FRONT ENDPAPERS: *Transylvanian lake • Seonna Hong, Hawaiian postcards • Joey Chou, Passport & 'color' photographs • Michael Kurinsky*
BACK ENDPAPERS: *Camp Winniepacaca • Aurora Jimenz*

Hotel Transylvania 2 TM & © 2015 Sony Pictures Animation Inc. All rights reserved.

ISBN: 9781783298815

Published by Titan Books, London, in 2015.

No part of this publication may be reproduced, stored in a retrieval system, or transmitted, in any form or by any means without the prior written permission of the publisher, nor be otherwise circulated in any form of binding or cover other than that in which it is published and without a similar condition being imposed on the subsequent purchaser.

TITAN BOOKS

A division of Titan Publishing Group Ltd
144 Southwark Street
London SE1 0UP
www.titanbooks.com

Find us on Facebook: www.facebook.com/titanbooks
Follow us on Twitter: @TitanBooks

A CIP catalogue record for this title is available from the British Library.

Printed and bound in China
10 9 8 7 6 5 4 3 2 1

PUBLISHER: *Chris Gruener*
CREATIVE DIRECTOR: *Iain R. Morris*
DESIGNERS: *Amy Wheless & Suzi Hutsell*
EDITOR: *Jake Gerli*
PROOFREADER: *Michelle Dotter*

Cameron + Company would like to thank Brett Rector for writing such a fun and in-depth book; Iain Morris for his original design and creative direction; Jake Gerli for his editorial guidance and expertise; Michelle Dotter for her proofreading skills; Virginia King and Sony Pictures Consumer Products, Melissa Sturm and everyone at Sony Pictures Animation for allowing us the honor of publishing this book.